The Star-Nosed Mole

William & Molly
with heartfelt thanks
for advice + support

The Star-Nosed Mole

An Anthology of
Scented Garden Writing

written and compiled by
Isabel Bannerman

Isabel.

PIMPERNEL
PRESS LTD
www.pimpernelpress.com

To go guided by fragrance is a hundred times better than following tracks.

Rumi (1207–1273) *The Granary Floor*

Pimpernel Press Limited
www.pimpernelpress.com

The Star-Nosed Mole
An Anthology of Scented Garden Writing
© Pimpernel Press Limited 2021
Introductory texts, editorial commentary and photographs
© Isabel Bannerman 2021
Please see page 144 for further copyright information

A catalogue record for this book is available from the British Library.

Designed by Dunstan Baker
www.greygray.co.uk
Typeset in Minion Pro

ISBN 978-1-910258-45-3

Printed and bound in China
by C&C Offset Printing Company

9 8 7 6 5 4 3 2 1

Contents

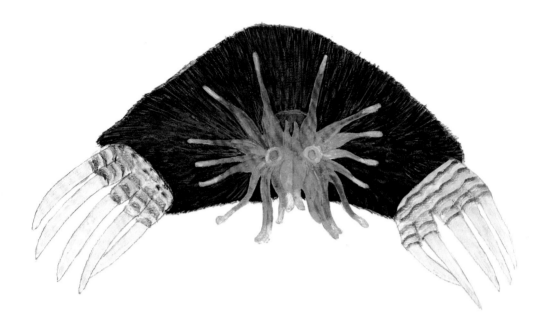

The Star-Nosed Mole

For my last book, 'Scent Magic' may not have been the best of titles, on reflection – when we were editing it I thought it should have been called 'Scent Mad' – but, as a title for a journal about growing and smelling plants in my garden, it locked in my belief in something supranatural about the magic of scent. Its powers are inestimable, not only for us, readers and gardeners, but for an extraordinary number of creatures and living organisms with whom we selfishly do not share this earth, but from whom we plunder and destroy its riches – including smell. I knew as a gardener with a passion for scent the obvious correlation between smell and pollination, that in some way scent existed to attract invertebrates. It was delicious to discover the processes that moths and butterflies apply to using scent as a guide in the dark – foraging, and scenting mates, as a much as 11 kilometres away. It was obvious, when I began to read about it, that in the reduced light, such as in woodland or underwater or underground, smell becomes a whole telegraphic system; that salmon follow scent in the seas and rivers; that shearwaters follow the smell of dimethyl sulphide (DMS) from plankton for their 8000-mile migrations; that bees signal in the frantically populous dark of the hive by emitting odours – as ants in their nests do, equally; and, only I had never thought of it, that moles navigate by smell in their damp dim world, 'Dreaming the flower I have never seen' (as Thom Gunn describes in 'Moly') while finding 'Cool flesh of magic in each leaf and shoot'.

I came across the star-nosed mole while writing about the riches of the soil kingdom, the teaming 'Underland', where more organisms thrive (or should thrive if it were not for us) than on land or in the sea. We know that moles are virtually blind and have huge fleshy paws for digging. Did we ever think about their tiny ears? Did we think about their noses? The mole sniffs out the worm in the dark; a hunter dressed in black velvet, a killing machine calculating the direction of prey stereoscopically, even though mole's nostrils are only millimetres apart. In studies, if the left nostril is blocked mole will go round and round to the right, and vice versa – thus missing the worm completely. But it would be difficult to close up one side of the star-nosed mole. A mole whom Edward Lear might have invented, this adorable and preposterous creature has a highly specialised sensory-motor organ shaped by 22 fleshy finger-like appendages that ring its nostrils, a unique touch organ with more than 25,000 tiny sensory receptors. The star-nosed mole is also able to smell underwater, exhaling air bubbles on to objects or scent trails, then inhaling the bubbles to carry scents back through the nose. Its nasal star and teeth appear to be primarily adapted to exploit extremely small prey, and the journal *Nature* calls it the fastest-eating mammal, since it takes as little as 120 milliseconds to identify and consume individual pieces of food. Its brain decides in approximately 8 milliseconds if a prey is edible or not – a speed at the limit of the speed of neurons.

These mysteries of the Underland in our gardens, fields, city streets show that scent has meaning and power by way of evolution. Plants and invertebrates co-evolved over the strands of time to construct an unbelievably sophisticated and complex web of co-existence using visual, tactile and odiferous clues and messages to attract, deter and communicate. Modern farming and gardening have done much to deplete the complex workings of our soil: the humus, the fungus, the mycorrhiza, the phylae, the bacteria, the soil organisms, the worms and so forth, that populate the hunting grounds of moles. But this Amazon jungle right here underfoot is barely explored. The dawning of some comprehension of that *richesse* made me call this book after *Condylura cristata*, the star-nosed mole, signifier of soil health, blind expert smeller.

The sense of smell is primal in a way we find hard to rationalise. We put it aside. But it always sneaks back, evoking memories, unlocking imagination, stirring the soul. We cannot help it – and rightly so. Smell from before we are born tells us telegraphically what we need to know, what is good for us and what is bad; attraction and aversion; kith and kin; edible or putrid; excrement or celestial ferment; disgust or delight; friend or foe (studies have shown that, following hand shaking, we sniff at our fingers repeatedly); flight or fight.

There is nothing quite like the smell of home. It reassures us. Conversely alien smells are at the heart of being away from home; if the *Umwelt* (see my Afterword) becomes unfamiliar it becomes threatening. That is how we are wired. Longing for home, having been lost in the wild wood, Mole in Kenneth Grahame's *The Wind in the Willows* (1908) unexpectedly catches a whiff of home. He experiences the ambush of scent, an emotional turmoil of the right thing in the wrong place.

> He stopped dead in his tracks, his nose searching hither and thither in its efforts to recapture the fine filament, the telegraphic current, that had so strongly moved him. A moment, and he had caught it again; and with it this time came recollection in fullest flood … Home! That was what they meant, those caressing appeals, those soft touches wafted through the air, those invisible little hands pulling and tugging, all one way!

Smell works overtime, a constant monitor of our *Umwelt*. The messages, minatory or uplifting, flow continuously on this subconscious level.

Somewhat mole-like, feeling blind and in a fog, with little academic knowledge, I began to nose about, questioning how others had conveyed smell in literature and natural history writing in the past. I am no scholar and there is no thesis, it only offers questions and some joyous surprises.

Introduction

I obsess about smell, hedonistically and emotionally. The sense of smell is a layer of experience somewhat blasted aside by its closely allied twin sense of taste, and the profoundly dominant vision, and perhaps – as almost nowhere is truly silent any more – the even more dominant auditory world. I became interested in whether smell is a diminishing experience. My reading for my book *Scent Magic – Notes from a Gardener* suggested that pollution, particulates, toxins and gases, actively destroy the fine volatiles detected by living organisms in the air and earth and sea. Pollution and distraction have ambushed our well-being. As I was trying to write about the impossibility of writing effectively about smell, I began to nose around for great writers' solutions to this problem. How and how much have writers considered the lilies of the field and how they smell. I began grazing on literature and gathering in my stores of quotes. For instance, in Jonathan Franzen's *Purity* I loved this passage: 'heaven … Two scents at once, distinct like layers of cooler and warmer water in a lake – some instantly flowering tropical tree's perfume, a complex lawn-smell from a pasture that goats were grazing – flooded through her open window. Heaven …'

In 2003 I had started making images of plants on my flatbed scanner. A very intense process which I tend to indulge in late at night, in the dark, which is how I discovered how to make it work. Making images with plants is a messy, sticky, visceral operation, all floating pollen and oozings. I have to keep the plants cool and work fast before they collapse. In the morning I often find my office, a small file-filled submarine, filled with scent. Many flowers emit more scent when stressed or dying in a last gasp for paternity. The pictures happened then, by a kind of accident and they seemed to have an ethereal otherness, a bit like scent. Another thing which ignited my inner child. I wanted to write a book about the uncanny feeling, the unsettling disorder, the subjective, the inadequacies of the intellect, the obscurity of intuition. These illustrations appear as an adjunct, but in fact they were the instigator of this quest because I was looking for a way to make the images have purpose, and at the same time I realised I wanted to write about gardening and smell. In the writing I did a lot of reading; it seems to me the big bonus about writing a book is that it gives you an excuse to read endless other books. And then quite recently, after the book was written, it seemed to me that the poetry and prose I was collecting was quite often in dialogue with the images. When I read that Baudelaire thought of himself as 'The poet of black' I thought how black my plant images are. And in reading 'Parisian Dream' could imagine no better description of the image on page 10.

> And every colour, even black,
> Became prismatic polished, bright;
> The liquid gave its glory back
> Mounted in iridescent light

The American poet Anthony Hecht said that 'Poetry operates by hints and dark suggestions. It is full of secrets and hidden formulae, like a witch's brew.' Smell is rather the same. It is the 'implied' sense, much of the time inferred subconsciously. Often, reading Emily Dickinson I feel smell is there but only by inference, of which she is queen. 'Autumn begins to be inferred' is one of my favourite lines, and I would argue that she is implying that we get the message first through the elusive smell of autumn (before autumn shows itself visually) when the year turns after the summer solstice – something I have monitored for ages. Peonies literally stop on the solstice; they harden and slowly die. In 'A Light Exists in Spring' Dickinson talks about light, but to me she is also implying scent … which also almost speaks to us.

> It waits upon the lawn;
> It shows the furthest tree
> Upon the furthest slope we know;
> It almost speaks to me.

But 'I Tend My Flowers for Thee' (1862) has a rare direct reference to smell.

> Carnations—tip their spice
> And Bees—pick up—
> A Hyacinth—I hid—
> Puts out a Ruffled Head—
> And odors fall
> From flasks—so small—
> You marvel how they held—.

Baudelaire also describes this mystery, this alchemy of smell in 'The Flask':

There are some powerful scents that can pass
Out of the stoppered flagon; even glass
To them is porous. Oft when some old box
Brought from the East is opened and the locks

And hinges creak and cry, or in a press
In some deserted house where the sharp stress
Of scents old and dusty fills the brain,
An ancient flask is brought to light again

And forth the ghosts of long-dead odours creep –
There, softly trembling in the shadows, sleep
A thousand thoughts, funereal chrysalides,
Phantoms of old the folding darkness hides,

Who make faint flutterings as their wings unfold,
Rose-washed and azure-tinted, shot with gold.
A memory that brings langour flutters here:
The fainting eyelids droop, and giddy fear …

So too, when vanished from man's memory
Deep in some dark and sombre chest I lie,
An empty flagon they have cast aside,
Broken and soiled, the dust upon my pride,

I'll be your shroud, beloved pestilence!
The witness of your might and virulence,
Sweet poison mixed by angels; bitter cup
Of life and death my heart has drunken up!

My images are, in part, about imagining smell. When Milton wrote in
Paradise Lost:

… off at sea north-east winds blow
Sabean odors, from the spicy shore
Of Araby the Blest; …

he did so without ever having been to the Yemen. He made it possible for his
readers to accompany him on his imaginary flight. There is an immediacy about
sixteenth- and seventeenth-century writing which we all recognise and admire.

An honesty too. I cannot abide the sort of coyness that infuses so much smell talk. Scent is primal, that is what fascinates. Some, such as Luca Turin, write honestly about smell and deal with the core expressed by Antonin Artaud that 'where there is the stink of shit there is a smell of being'. Our fear of the stink of shit, extraordinarily smelly stuff, loaded with sulphur, our disgust, has been an adaptation, biologically rooted, part of our behavioural immune system that evolved to keep us from encountering infection and disease, tweaked and tuned by culture and social conditioning only in very recent history.

What makes the heart leap and breathing quicken? Twilight; the gone summers; butterflies; moths; sensuality; synaesthesia; perception; olfaction; balance and ecology; catastrophe and the groping for meaning – all well up and beg for attention. How enriching would it be to attend to these questions. Age diminishes the senses. Sight, hearing, touch, taste and, by equal degrees, smell evaporate, depart, harden, muffle and dim. We live in a constantly altering state, swimming in flows and currents of perception, much of which is invisible or goes unnoticed. To take time now to analyse a minuscule, highly personal, bandwidth of all that vastness of experience, to shine a small beam and encourage the hedonic pleasures of smelling and reading what others have smelled became my mission.

Before last Christmas I employed Violet Hudson to help collate all the scraps of literature, prose, poetry and garden writing that I had garnered while writing *Scent Magic* (and which Sarah Mitchell, my editor, had pruned from it) and together with Dunstan Baker we put them into some sort of seasonal order, married up with my plant images and made a small commonplace book of smelly thoughts to cheer a few friends through the coming dark days. Jo Christian at Pimpernel Press offered to publish an expanded version and away we went in a torrid scramble to get something print-ready by April.

What have others thought about this underrated, ugly duckling sense? It's hard to tell. Pictures and made things tell us little about scent – apart from specific use things like thuribles and incense burners which tell of great worth by their great workmanship. Only the written word, several thousand years' worth, can perhaps indicate answers to the questions that arose during the writing of *Scent Magic*; did things smell stronger in the past? If, as I think you will agree, the writing here suggests this is so, have we lost interest or is our sense of smell genuinely depleted? If so, is this having not only a disheartening effect on our psyches, but a detrimental effect upon the balanced workings of the natural world? The small amount of research that seems to have been done on this subject, and even smaller amount studied by me on the web and reading the likes of Dave Goulson, would suggest that smell volatiles are decimated by the pollution of the air since the industrial revolution, which initially only affected the microcosms of developed industry, but now affect an enormous proportion of the globe. This decimation is almost certainly detrimental to the reproductive processes of invertebrates, their foraging and mating, their associative and inadvertent acts of pollination, and hence is likely to be a factor, I would argue, in the catastrophic collapse of invertebrates that we are witnessing.

Violet and I are, we realise, on a lifelong rummage now; never again will we read a novel or a poem without our antennae twitching at the whiff of a smell simile. We have but nibbled at the edges of this particular mushroom, like the caterpillar in *Alice in Wonderland*. What a delightful bite it has been. Perhaps it made all the difference in getting through this particular winter. Turning to William Sieghart's *Poetry Pharmacy*, where the deftly handled advice and suggested poetic sources of solace provided a strong starting point, it dawned on me that the process of reading poetry is indeed healing, reflective and uplifting. Racing through *The New Penguin Book of English Verse* (brilliantly edited by Paul Keegan) I felt like an aurelian dancing over sweet meadows in search of elusive butterflies. I think the crocks of beauty we bit-mined helped all of us to 'winter this one out' and, thank you, Seamus Heaney and all the writers here and not in here for yes, now 'we can summer anywhere'.

Here is a book to pluck and pick through, to find all this 'juice, this joy' in words and images. The animadversions on my part are an attempt to link the story, such as it is, and to reflect upon what it all might reveal about the question of our real impoverishment. The lesson not learnt from Silas Marner, that bitcoin brings no nourishment, and yet the so called 'mining' of the ultimate emperor's new gold is using the equivalent power resources of the whole of Argentina. This is obscene. There are many obscene things done by humankind, to each other mostly, abhorrent and inhumane, but perhaps it is worth sparing a small moment of our self-centred lives to consider the lilies, and the lily beetles. How this world was refined, bit by selective bit, to construct a wonder web of a safety net, mostly invisible to our gawkish eyes, infinitely balanced and checked, giving and taking, reciprocating, facilitating others by symbiosis and a self-interested altruism. Scent plays its invisible part, has played its crucial part in this slow construction long, long before we existed. It continued and it continues to sing silently with all the natural world. Smell chemistry is just one strand that we need to understand, and we have the capacity. Read these pages of abundance and solace; imagine the nard, the ambergris – things most of us will never actually smell; remember jasmine, the balms, the incense from arabic gums and all these miracles of nature, and wonder why do we so thoughtlessly plunder? Read these pages and disagree. Something beyond magic, some physics, some chemistry, some biology we have barely noticed is being lost. Fast. We need to act.

Christmas

The thing about Christmas is that it is a druidic festival again, now that most of us are not Christians. It is about bringing branches and foliage indoors and gathering round the home fire to confirm that together we will get out the other side of the dark days and Phoebus and Persephone will return. The smell of the Christmas tree and the smells of all the accoutrements of Christmas get lodged in our psyche from an early age. It is of course also bound up with feasting and Nigel Slater is incredibly good on these delights and memories in his *Christmas Chronicles*. '… if by any chance you come downstairs during the night, you will be met with the citrus-pine note of freshly cut Christmas tree. A smell that is both ancient and fresh, clean and homely. The scent of forests and snow.' Tangerines for me are quintessential; that explosion of clementine volatiles sparking at the peeling of the booty at the very bottom of the lumpy woolly shooting socks my father used for our Christmas stockings – he did not shoot but his mother must have given him quite a supply of them for five children. Katherine Mansfield writes from France 'The air smells of faint, far-off tangerines with just a touch of nutmeg.' I love Mollie Panter-Downes' observations such as this one on winter smells: 'The air was peppermint cold in the nostrils … there was a bitter earthy smell in the woods as though the lees of the year had been stirred and left to settle under a scum of withered bryony in the ditches.'

The sun was shining very brightly and even London looked pretty. Women were selling roses from big baskets-full, and Anthea bought four roses, one each, for herself and the others. They were red roses and smelt of summer – the kind of roses you always want so desperately at about Christmastime when you can only get mistletoe, which is pale right through to its very scent, and holly which pricks your nose if you try to smell it.

E. Nesbit *The Story of the Amulet* (1906)

The holly in the windy hedge
And round the Manor House the yew
Will soon be stripped to deck the ledge,
The altar, font and arch and pew,
So that the villagers can say
'The church looks nice' on Christmas Day …
And London shops on Christmas Eve
Are strung with silver bells and flowers
As hurrying clerks the City leave
To pigeon-haunted classic towers,
And marbled clouds go scudding by
The many-steepled London sky …

And is it true? For if it is,
No loving fingers tying strings
Around those tissued fripperies,
The sweet and silly Christmas things,
Bath salts and inexpensive scent
And hideous tie so kindly meant …
Can with this single Truth compare …

John Betjeman 'Christmas' (1954)

The midnight chant had helped as usual to lift the morning above the level of common days; and then there was the smell of hot toast and ale from the kitchen at breakfast hour; the favourite anthem, the green boughs and the short sermon, gave the appropriate festal character to the church-going …

George Eliot *The Mill on the Floss* (1860)

Heap on more wood! — the wind is chill;
But let it whistle as it will,
We'll keep our Christmas merry still.
Each age has deemed the new born year
The fittest time for festal cheer ...
The hail was dressed with holly green;
Forth to the wood did merry men go,
To gather in the mistletoe ...
All hailed with uncontroll'd delight
And general voice, the happy night
That to the cottage, as the crown,
Brought tidings of salvation down.
The fire with well dried logs supplied,
Went roaring up the chimney wide; ...
England was merry England when
Old Christmas brought his sports again.
'Twas Christmas broached the mightiest ale,
'Twas Christmas told the merriest tale;
A Christmas gambol oft would cheer
A poor man's heart through half the year.

Walter Scott (1771–1832) 'Christmas in the Olden Time'

Come, then, my men,
To pluck wild garlic,
To pluck wild garlic,
And, on our road,
The fragrant-scented
Orange tree in flower ...

Attrib. to Emperor Ōjin of Japan (*c.*270–*c.*310) 'Song of Proposal'

Oranges in tissue paper packed in crates. Citrons too ... Nice to hold, cool waxen fruit, hold in the hand, lift it to the nostrils and smell the perfume. Like that, heavy, sweet, wild perfume. Always the same, year after year.

James Joyce *Ulysses* (1922)

Deep Winter
January

Nigel Slater, again in his *Christmas Chronicles*, takes us to Sorrento on a breath of orange blossom '… preferably caught on a breeze rather than from a bottle. (Too much, it reminds me of Savlon, and childhood grazes and cuts.) If ever you are in Sorrento in Italy in the winter, head for the nearest lemon tree, often overhanging the path, and its white, star-like blossom. There is an olfactory treat in store.' Slater is good on how the paucity of smell when it is cold, makes the slightest whiff much more intense. Scented winter plants are cherished because of their rarity and bravery. And his notion of winter is also always homely and cheering in the smell department because he is cooking something delicious indoors. 'Scent always seems particularly intense to me in winter. The smell of toasted crumpet on a frosty morning. The sap from a branch, snapped in the garden, or of lemon zest grated in the kitchen, all seem especially vivid, heightened at this time of year. The cold air seems to illuminate scent … Some things actually smell cold. Snow, obviously, but also peppermint, cucumber, yoghurt, ginger and juniper.' Cucumber as a winter smell is very Russian. though Anton Chekhov, in 'A Lady's Story' (1899), has a character maintain that '… when one eats fresh cucumbers in winter there is the fragrance of spring in one's mouth.' Or again, like Slater's sap from a branch, in 'After the Theatre' (1892) Chekhov's heroine '… had a passionate longing for the garden, the darkness, the pure sky, the stars. Again her shoulders shook with laughter, and it seemed to her that there was a scent of wormwood in the room and that a twig was tapping at the window.' In his *Natural History* (AD 77) Pliny the Elder also commends a smell: 'As for the garden mint, the very smell of it alone recovers and refreshes our spirits.'

Farewell, Life! My senses swim,
And the world is growing dim;
Thronging shadows cloud the light,
Like the advent of the night –
Colder, colder, colder still,
Upward steals a vapour chill;
Strong the earthy odour grows –
I smell the mould above the rose!

Welcome, Life! the spirit strives:
Strength returns, and hope revives;
Cloudy fears and shapes forlorn
Fly like shadows at the morn –
O'er the earth there comes a bloom:
Sunny light for sullen gloom,
Warm perfume for vapour cold –
I smell the rose above the mould!

Thomas Hood (1799–1845) 'Farewell, Life!'

Masked by the snowflakes,
The colour of your petals
May well be hidden:
Yet still put forth your scent
That men may know you flower.

Ono Takamura (*c*.802–853)

Soon, trembling in her soft and chilly nest,
In sort of wakeful swoon, perplex'd she lay,
Until the poppied warmth of sleep oppress'd
Her soothed limbs, and soul fatigued away;
Flown, like a thought, until the morrow-day;
Blissfully haven'd both from joy and pain;
Clasp'd like a missal where swart Paynims pray;
Blinded alike from sunshine and from rain,
As though a rose should shut, and be a bud again ...

And still she slept an azure-lidded sleep,
In blanched linen, smooth, and lavender'd,
While he forth from the closet brought a heap
Of candied apple, quince, and plum, and gourd;
With jellies soother than the creamy curd,
And lucent syrops, tinct with cinnamon;
Manna and dates, in argosy transferr'd
From Fez; and spiced dainties, every one,
From silken Samarcand to cedar'd Lebanon.

These delicates he heap'd with glowing hand
On golden dishes and in baskets bright
Of wreathed silver: sumptuous they stand
In the retired quiet of the night,
Filling the chilly room with perfume light.—
"And now, my love, my seraph fair, awake!
Thou art my heaven, and I thine eremite:
Open thine eyes, for meek St. Agnes' sake,
Or I shall drowse beside thee, so my soul doth ache." ...

Beyond a mortal man impassion'd far
At these voluptuous accents, he arose
Ethereal, flush'd, and like a throbbing star
Seen mid the sapphire heaven's deep repose;
Into her dream he melted, as the rose
Blendeth its odour with the violet,
Solution sweet: meantime the frost-wind blows
Like Love's alarum pattering the sharp sleet
Against the windowpanes; St. Agnes' moon hath set.

John Keats 'The Eve of St Agnes' (1819)

In Nature's poem flowers have each their word
The rose of love and beauty sings alone;
The violet's soul exhales in tenderest tone;
The lily's one pure simple note is heard.
The cold Camellia only, stiff and white,
Rose without perfume, lily without grace,
When chilling winter shows his icy face,
Blooms for a world that vainly seeks delight.
Yet, in a theatre, or ball-room light,
With alabaster petals opening fair,
I gladly see Camellias shining bright
Above some stately woman's raven hair,
Whose noble form fulfils the heart's desire,
Like Grecian marbles warmed by Phidian fire.

Honoré de Balzac 'The Camellia' (from *Illusions Perdues*, 1843)

Midwinter Spring
February

In 'Little Gidding', T. S. Eliot writes that midwinter spring is its own time of year: 'In the dark time of the year … The soul's sap quivers. There is no earth smell …' This last February there came a mean frozen wind from the Urals and, with a certain amount of thrill we stoked up the fires and were amazed at the pleasantness of dry cold. It was only with the thaw, when a balmy springy cow-patty smell oozed all round the lanes here, that I realised how scent-less the past week had been on account of the low temperature and the low humidity which had prevented that background earth smell, a thing we take for granted and barely register normally, from emanating at all. Earth smells recur in literature, grounding and vital; in Paris, John Montague would '… smell the earth of the garden … It exhales softly, … Especially now, approaching springtime …'

February smells like the end of the gardener's world, but then it begins to feel like the end of the end of the world. New horizons open up, the sun's risings and settings creep in a northerly direction and the days stretch hesitantly. Violets and 'willows start to peep', as John Evelyn put it. And also wintersweet, which is possibly my favourite plant and flower smell, which Vita Sackville-West describes as 'Waxen, Chinese and drooping bell … Strange in its colour, almond in its smell', although I would call the smell a profoundly intense shimmering jasmine.

They walked over the crackling leaves in the garden, between the lines of box, breathing its fragrance of eternity; for this is one of the odors which carry us out of time into the abysses of the unbeginning past; if we ever lived on another ball of stone than this, it must be that there was box growing on it.

Oliver Wendell Holmes (1809–1894)

There had once been a flowerbed in it, and she thought she saw something sticking out of the black earth – some sharp little pale green points … 'Yes, they are tiny growing things, and they might be crocuses or snowdrops or daffodils,' she whispered. She bent very close to them and sniffed the fresh scent of the damp earth. She liked it very much.

Frances Hodgson Burnett *The Secret Garden* (1911)

In the days of my early youth a vast clump … of evergreens occupied the space which now forms my home for demented plants. It was the sort of planting one sees at one end of a London square. Portugal Laurels there were, and the still more objectionable Common Laurel; bushes which in showery weather exhale an odour of a dirty dog kennel and an even dirtier dog; …

E. A. Bowles *My Garden in Spring* (1914)

The snowdrop gives me chilblains only to look at it – and the very sigh of a snowdrop will always make me hurry to the fireside. Was there ever such an icy, inhuman bloodless flower, crystallised winter in three gleaming petals and green-flecked cup?

Reginald Farrer *In A Yorkshire Garden* (1909)

The Snow-drop, Winter's timid child,
Awakes to life, bedew'd with tears,
And flings around its fragrance mild;
And where no rival flow'rets blooms,
Amid the bare and chilling gloom.
A beauteous gem appears! …

Mary Robinson (1758–1800) 'Ode to the Snow-drop'

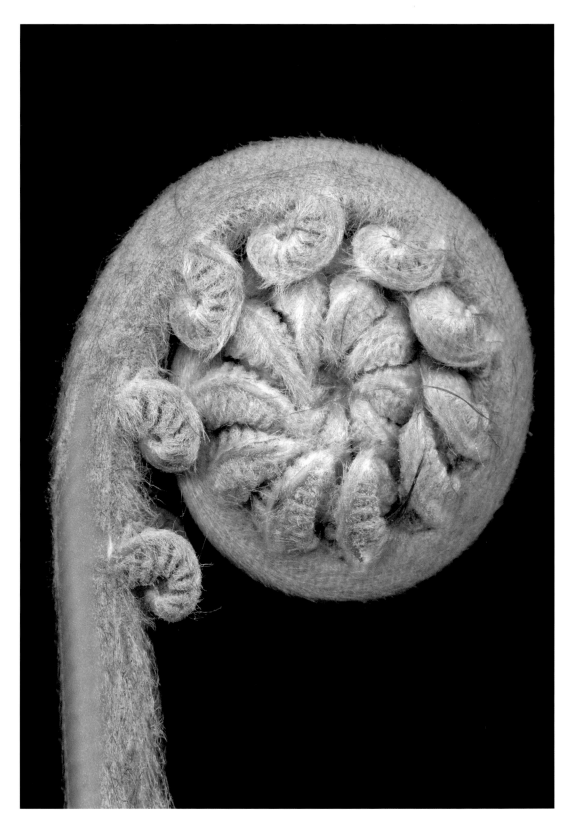

I liked … the great basins full of white hyacinths, all their cones of bells evenly grown together, not one mature beyond another. There was a second scent behind the rich penetration of the hyacinths … In a long shallow glass box stephanotis lay among its leather leaves. I smelt it, and it breathed out at me like an animal.

Molly Keane *Good Behaviour* (1981)

I dreamed that, as I wandered by the way,
Bare Winter suddenly was changed to Spring,
And gentle odours led my steps astray,
Mixed with a sound of waters murmuring
Along a shelving bank of turf, which lay
Under a copse, and hardly dared to fling
Its green arms round the bosom of the stream,
But kissed it and then fled, as thou mightest in dream.

Percy Bysshe Shelley (1792–1822) 'The Question'

Nature's First Green Is Gold
March

Robert Frost describes this moment – it is happening now as I write – when the first golden slivers of willow and alder break. When you might just catch a waft of early balsam poplar and all sticky buds, busy being harvested for propolis by bees. Daffodils naturally spring to mind, even in dusty city streets, as in Frances Cornford's poem 'London Spring' (1948):

The rounded buses loom through softest blue,
The pavement smells of dust but of narcissus too,
The awnings stretch like petals in the sun,
And even the oldest taxis glitter as they run.

Over the sooted secret garden walls
As in another Eden cherry-blossom falls,
Lithe under shadowing lilacs steal the cats,
And even the oldest ladies tilt their summery hats.

All towns perk up in the spring. Katherine Mansfield, though, found that the scent of bought daffodils palled: '… And the grossness of everything. I can't stand the narcissi even. I feel there are too many and the scent is too cheap,' she wrote to Ottoline Morell. One can feel when reading Mansfield that all her experience of life was intensified by the dark knowledge that her consumption would most likely cut her life short, and this heightened state of awareness made her writing sing: '… this room smells spicy and sweet from the carnations – pink and red and wonderful yellow. The hyacinths, in a big jar are put on the windowsill for the night for my little maid says they give you not only sore throats but dreams as well! … I have spent days just walking about or sitting on a stone in the sun and listening to the bees in the almond trees and the wild pear bushes and coming home in the evening with rosemary on my fingers and wild thyme on my toes – tired out with the loveliness of the world.'

Tarana Street was beautiful in the spring; there was not a single house without its garden and trees and a plot of grass big enough to be called 'the lawn.' Over the low painted fences, you could see, as you ran by, whose daffys were out, whose wild snowdrop border was over and who had the biggest hyacinths, so pink and white, the colour of cocoanut ice. But nobody had violets that grew, that smelled in the spring sun like Bengel's. Did they really smell like that? Or did you shut your eyes and lean over the fence because of Edie Bengel's piano?

A little wind ruffles among the leaves like a joyful hand looking for the finest flowers; and the piano says gay, tender, laughing. Now a cloud, like a swan, flies across the sun, the violets shine cold, like water … Ah, if life must pass quickly, why is the breath of these flowers so sweet? What is the meaning of this feeling of longing, of sweet trouble – of flying joy? Goodbye! Farewell! The young bees lie half-awake on the slender dandelions, silver are the pink tipped arrowy petals of the daisies; the new grass shakes in the light. Everything is beginning again, marvellous as ever, heavenly fair.

Katherine Mansfield *Weak Heart* (1923)

O the green things growing, the green things growing,
The faint sweet smell of the green things growing!

Dinah Mulock Craik 'Green Things' (1881)

When daffodils begin to peer,
With heigh! the doxy over the dale,
Why, then comes in the sweet o' the year;
For the red blood reigns in the winter's pale.

The white sheet bleaching on the hedge,
With heigh! the sweet birds, O, how they sing!
Doth set my pugging tooth on edge;
For a quart of ale is a dish for a king.

The lark, that tirra-lyra chants,
With heigh! with heigh! the thrush and the jay,
Are summer songs for me and my aunts,
While we lie tumbling in the hay.

Shakespeare *The Winter's Tale* (c.1611)

'Twas early summer, and the sunshine flooded her from head to foot; the window and balcony were full of flowers – yellow jonquils and daffodils, white narcissus, and all things fragrant of the spring. The scent of them floated about her like an incense, and a straying zephyr blew great puffs of their sweetness back into the room.

Frances Hodgson Burnett *A Lady of Quality* (1896)

When the east wind blows,
Send me your perfume,
Blossoms of the plum:
Though your lord be absent,
Forget not the spring.

Sugawara Michizane (AD 845–903)

Still to taste the warm sunlight that melted in your mouth; still to smell the white waxy scent that lay upon the jonquil fields and the wild spicy scent of the rosemary growing in little tufts among the red rocks close to the brim of the sea …

Katherine Mansfield 'Et in Arcadia Ego' (*Journal*, 1919)

… jonquil fair
That sweet perfumer of the evening air
… Should there be seen with tufts of smelling musk
The woodbine tree should all her sweets unfurl
Close to my door in many a wanton curl …

John Clare (1793–1864) 'The Wish'

The wind swept in soft big breaths down from the moor and was strange with a wild clear scented sweetness. Colin kept lifting his thin chest to draw it in, and his big eyes looked as if it were they which were listening – listening, instead of his ears. 'There are so many sounds of singing and humming and calling out,' he said. 'What is that scent the puffs of wind bring?' 'It's gorse on th' moor that's openin' out,' answered Dickon. 'Eh! Th' bees are at it wonderful today.'

Frances Hodgson Burnett *The Secret Garden* (1911)

The scent of the gorse on the moors drove me wild, and the primroses under the hedges.

R. D. Blackmore *Lorna Doone* (1869)

… Miles of pram in the wind and Pam in the gorse track,
Coco-nut smell of the broom, and a packet of Weights
Press'd in the sand. The thud of hoof on horse-track-
A horse-riding horse for a horse-track-
Conifer county of Surrey approached
Through remarkable wrought-iron gates.
… I will take the slippery third path
Trodden away with gym shoes,
Beautiful fir-dry alley that leads
To the bountiful body of Pam …
Over the redolent pinewoods, in at the bathroom casement,
One fine Saturday, Windlesham bells shall call:
Up the Butterfield aisle rich with Gothic enlacement,
Licensed now for embracement,
Pam and I, as the organ
Thunders over you all.

John Betjeman 'Pot Pourri from A Surrey Garden' (1940)

And over walls and earth and trees and swinging sprays and tendrils the fair green veil of tender little leaves had crept, and in the grass under the trees and the gray urns in the alcoves and here and there everywhere were touches or splashes of gold and purple and white and the trees were showing pink and snow above his head and there was a fluttering of wings and faint sweet pipes and humming and scents and scents. And the sun fell warm upon his face like a hand with a lovely touch.

Frances Hodgson Burnett *The Secret Garden* (1911)

Like the wild hyacinth flower which on the hills is found,
Which the passing feet of the shepherds for ever tear and wound,
Until the purple blossom is trodden into the ground.

Sappho (*c.*630–570 BC) Poem 105a, trans. Dante Gabriel Rossetti

And the hyacinth purple, white and blue
Which flung from its bells a sweet peel anew
Of music so delicate, soft and intense,
It was felt like an odour within the sense.

Percy Bysshe Shelley (1792–1822) 'The Sensitive Plant'

The greenhouse was not far off, and these words brought us to it. It contained quite a show of beautiful geraniums. We loitered along in front of them … and if we were not all three in Fairyland, certainly I was. The scent of a geranium leaf, at this day, strikes me with a half comical half serious wonder as to what change has come over me in a moment; and then I see a straw hat and blue ribbons, and a quantity of curls, and a little black dog being held up, in two slender arms, against a bank of blossoms and bright leaves.

Charles Dickens *David Copperfield* (1850)

My windows are gay with hyacinths and lilies of the valley; and though, as I have said, I don't admire the smell of hyacinths in the spring when it seems wanting in youth and chastity next to that of other flowers, I am glad enough now to bury my nose in their heavy sweetness …

Elizabeth von Arnim *Elizabeth and her German Garden* (1898)

Violets and Mimosa

Violet Group – this is the elusive and nose-fatiguing group; eagerness does not pay off, for you cannot grasp these smells by sniffing assiduously. Perversely the exquisite scent of the violet is not born of a desire to attract pollinators, for they pollinate themselves. Perhaps for this reason the distinctive smell is there still in all parts of the plant, roots and leaves as well as flowers, and it is the last word in subtlety, having a cool mossy quality unlike any other flower. Something like it can be found in *Iris reticulata*, in vine flowers, mimosa and the white banksian rose. The impression is that of a single sweetness shading off through something almost resembling cedar wood, which is ferny and mossy. So delicious. In this case the smell is coming from esters and ketones, ionone in the violet and in the closely smell related orris root *irone*. The origins of mimosa, or *Acacia farnesiana*, are uncertain but it is found in both Africa and as silver or blue wattle all over Australia; it is called by French perfumiers 'cassie', and has two detectable principal notes, which are hawthorn and violet. Celia Lyttelton in her magical odyssey Into the realms of smell, *The Scent Trail*, writes 'Demand [for mimosa] was such that a special train left Menton to get large quantities for the florists of Paris – valued for its fougère fern-like woodland scent and for its spicy floral notes, nor is it delicate but rather it is warm and earthy and full of buttery pulverence … golden, honeyed, summery, dry, earthy, with an oleaginous sweetness.' And Katherine Mansfield, acerbic as ever, catches the feel of mimosa-lined streets in the South of France in this stanza from 'Sanary' (1916)

> … Down below at this idle hour
> Nobody walked in the dusty street
> A scent of dying mimosa flower
> Lay on the air, but sweet – too sweet.

But if you should forget, then I will remind you
How fair and good were the things we shared together,
How by my side you wove many garlands of violets and
Sweet-smelling roses, and made of all kinds of flowers
Delicate necklaces, how many a flask of the finest myrrh
Such as a king might use you poured on your body,
How then reclining you sipped the sweet drinks of your choice.

Sappho (*c.* 7th century BC) trans. Richard Aldington

Recently fallen, still with wings out,
she spoke her name to summon us to her darkness.

Not wanting to be seen, but not uncurious
She spoke her name and let her purple deep eye-pupil be peered into.

'Violet,' she said
and showed her heart under its leaf.

Then she leant a little frightened forwards
And picked a hand to pick her.

And her horrified mouseface, sniffed and lifted close,
Let its gloom be taken and all the sugar licked off its strangeness

While we all stood there saying, 'Violet! Violet!'
Fingering her blue bruised skin.

Finally she mentioned
The name of her name

Which was something so pin-sharp,
In such a last gasp of a previously unknown language,

It could only be spoken as a scent,
It could only be heard as our amazement.

Alice Oswald 'Violet' (2009)

The forward violet thus did I chide:
Sweet thief, whence didst thou steal thy sweet that smells,
If not from my love's breath? …

William Shakespeare (1564–1616) Sonnet 99

Love on a day, wise poets tell,
Some time in wrangling spent,
Whether the violets should excel,
Or she, in sweetest scent.

But Venus having lost the day,
Poor girls, she fell on you:
And beat ye so, as some dare say,
Her blows did make ye blue.

Robert Herrick (1591–1674) 'How Violets Came Blue'

Sweetly breathing, vernal air,
That with kind warmth doth repair
Winter's ruins; from whose breast
All the gums and spice of the East
Borrow their perfumes; whose eye
Gilds the morn, and clears the sky.
Whose dishevelled tresses shed
Pearls upon the violet bed;
On whose brow, with calm smiles drest
The halcyon sits and builds her nest;
Beauty, youth, and endless spring
Dwell upon thy rosy wing!

Thomas Carew (1595–1639) 'The Seasons'

The violets whisper from the shade
Which their own leaves have made:
Men scent our fragrance on the air,
Yet take no heed
Of humble lessons we would read.

Christina Rossetti 'Consider the Lilies of the Field' (1879)

Who can say
Why To-day
To-morrow will be yesterday?
Who can tell
Why to smell
The violet, recalls the dewy prime
Of youth and buried time?
The cause is nowhere found in rhyme?

Alfred, Lord Tennyson (1809–1892) 'Who Can Say?'

For the moment, the sunshine fell brightly into the churchyard, there was a vague scent of sap and of spring, perhaps of violets from off the graves. Some white daisies were out, bright as angels. In the air, the unfolding leaves of a copper-beech were blood-red.

D. H. Lawrence *Women in Love* (1920)

Lilac-Tide
April

For John Gerard (1545–1612) lilac was 'too sweet, troubling and molesting the head in a very strange way'. Perhaps coming in the cruellest month, breeding lilacs out of the dead land, it elicits very opposite reactions. As with Horace Walpole and Hamish Bowles, lilac is the thing for me and Mr B. We love the memory-invoking qualities of this singular smell, a smell full of indole. This is the mysterious and powerful scent associated with faeces when not in dilution, but when perfectly balanced with other notes it is responsible for the allure of the most compulsive smells: jonquils, orange blossom and mock orange. These are smells that mix memory and desire as Eliot puts it in *The Wasteland*, 'stirring dull roots with spring rain'.

Gardening for Horace Walpole, as for myself and Mr B, amounted to hope, promise, anticipation, longing, nostalgia and loss and in March 1765 he writes of 'holding off' a trip to Paris in order to stay at Strawberry Hill for the magic moment of lilac-tide. His deepest ardour was for lilac, to which he returned each season like the nightingales. In March 1766 Horace's anticipation was all the more intense. 'Lilac-tide approaches, and I long as much to see a bit of green as a housemaid does that stick a piece of mint in a dirty phial.' Lilac-tide was a constant for Horace, reliable through the vicissitudes of his gardening life; he made sure to be at Strawberry Hill at this time 'where my two passions Lilacs and Nightingales are in full bloom'. But always the master of lilac-tide, after Walpole, is Proust.

Before reaching it we would be met on our way by the scent of his lilac-trees, come out to welcome strangers. Out of the fresh little green hearts of their foliage the lilacs raised inquisitively over the fence of the park their plumes of white or purple blossom, which glowed, even in the shade, with the sunlight in which they had been bathed … The nymphs of spring would have seemed coarse and vulgar in comparison with these young houris, who retained, in this French garden, the pure and vivid colouring of a Persian miniature. Despite my desire to throw my arms about their pliant forms and to draw down towards me the starry locks that crowned their fragrant heads, we would pass them by without stopping … Lilac-time was nearly over; some of the trees still thrust aloft, in tall purple chandeliers, their tiny balls of blossom, but in many places among their foliage where, only a week before, they had still been breaking in waves of fragrant foam, these were now spent and shrivelled and discoloured, a hollow scum, dry and scentless.

Marcel Proust *Swann's Way* (1913)

… oh, those lilac bushes! They are all out today, and the garden is drenched with the scent. I have brought in armfuls, the picking is such a delight, and every pot and bowl and tub in the house is filled with purple glory, and the servants think there is going to be a party and are extra nimble, and I go from room to room gazing at the sweetness, and the windows are all flung open so as to join the scent within to the scent without; and the servants gradually discover that there is no party, and wonder why the house should be filled with flowers for one woman by herself …

Elizabeth von Arnim *Elizabeth and her German Garden* (1898)

Sweet is the scent of the hawthorn, and sweet are the bluebells that hide in the valley, and the heather that blows on the hill.

Oscar Wilde 'The Nightingale and the Rose' (from *The Happy Prince and Other Tales*, 1888)

And meanwhile the beautiful golden days were dropping gently from the second week one by one, equal in beauty with those of the first, and the scent of beanfields in flower on the hillside behind the village came across to San Salvatore whenever the air moved. In the garden that second week the poet's eyed narcissus disappeared out of the long grass at the edge of the zigzag path, and the wild gladiolus, slender and rose-coloured, came in their stead, white pinks bloomed in the borders, filling the whole place with their smoky-sweet smell, and a bush nobody had noticed burst into glory and fragrance, and it was a purple lilac bush.

Elizabeth von Arnim *The Enchanted April* (1922)

All down the stone steps on either side were periwinkles in full flower, and she could now see what it was that had caught at her the night before and brushed, wet and scented, across her face. It was wisteria. Wisteria and sunshine … The wisteria was tumbling over itself in its excess of life, its prodigality of flowering.

Elizabeth von Arnim *The Enchanted April* (1922)

Lusty Hawthorn & Blossom
May

Call me sentimental but I do like this bit about cowslips from 'In the Botanical Gardens' (1907) by Katherine Mansfield

> … In the enclosure the spring flowers are almost too beautiful – a great stretch of foam-like cowslips. As I bend over them, the air is heavy and sweet with their scent, like hay and new milk and the kisses of children …

So much is going on In May that it's hard to keep up. May blossom is categorised in smell terms as in the aminoid group. These smells are sweet but stale and stinky even when dilute. Here we are into the realm of sperm. Hawthorn's smell quality is due to anisic aldehyde, found in many of the genera Rosaceae, *Crataegus* (hawthorn, May-tree) foremost among them. Hawthorn is thought to be desperately unlucky cut and arranged inside the house, where is does not smell pleasant, but dissolved upon the air in lanes and meadows it is the lusty smell of spring. Others in the family flower around now, smelling similar: *Sorbus, Pyrus, Cotoneaster, Spirea, Sambucus, Viburnum* and privet – all of them deeply suburban, Proustian, not to say Pooterish. I love the smell of hawthorn and all that it encapsulates, the high octane of the year. For Proust and Catholic France, May is the month of Mary the mother of Christ, and her feasts are bound up with the smell of all blossom and most particularly *muguet*, or lily of the valley (*Convallaria majalis*), which it is traditional to give to your lover or mother on the first of May.

When before turning to leave the church, I made a genuflection before the altar, I felt suddenly, as I rose again, a bitter-sweet fragrance of almonds steal towards me from the hawthorn-blossom, and then I noticed that the flowers themselves were little spots of a creamier colour, in which I imagined that this fragrance must lie concealed, as the taste of an almond cake lay in the burned parts, or the sweetness of Madamoiselle Vinteuil's cheeks beneath their freckles. Despite the heavy, motionless silence of the hawthorns, these gusts of fragrance came to me like the murmuring of an intense vitality, with which the whole altar was quivering like a roadside hedge explored by living antennae, of which I was reminded by seeing some stamens, almost red in colour, which seemed to have kept the springtime virulence, the irritant power of stinging insects now transmuted into flowers … I found the whole path throbbing with the fragrance of hawthorn blossom. The hedge resembled a series of chapels, whose walls were no longer visible under the mountains of flowers that were heaped upon their altars; while underneath the sun cast a square of lights upon the ground, as though I had been standing before the Lady-altar, and the flowers, themselves adorned also, held out each its little bunch of glittering stamens with an air of inattention, fine, radiating 'nerves' in the flamboyant style of architecture … But it was in vain that I lingered before the hawthorns, to breathe in, to marshal before my mind (which knew not what to make of it), to lose in order to rediscover their invisible and unchanging odour, to absorb myself in the rhythm which disposed their flowers here and there with the light-heartedness of youth, and at intervals as unexpected as certain intervals of music; they offered me an indefinite continuation of the same charm, in an inexhaustible profusion, but without letting me delve into it any more deeply, like those melodies which one can play over a hundred times in succession without coming any nearer to their secret … I returned to the hawthorns, and stood before them as one stands before those masterpieces of painting which, one imagines, one will be better able to 'take in' when one has looked away, for a moment, at something …

Marcel Proust *Swann's Way* (1913)

With enchanting murmurs Daisy admired this aspect or that of the feudal silhouette against the sky, admired the gardens, the sparkling odor of jonquils and the frothy odor of hawthorn and plum blossoms and the pale gold odor of kiss-me-at-the-gate.

F. Scott Fitzgerald *The Great Gatsby* (1925)

The cowslips tall her pensioners be;
In their gold coats spots you see;
Those be rubies, fairy favours,
In those freckles live their savours:
I must go seek some dewdrops here,
And hang a pearl in every cowslip's ear.

William Shakespeare *A Midsummer Night's Dream* (1595/6)

Now the bright morning Star, Dayes harbinger,
Comes dancing from the East, and leads with her
The flowry May, who from her green lap throws
The yellow Cowslip and the pale Primrose.

Milton 'Song on May Morning' (1645)

Little brings the May breeze
Beside pure scent of flowers,
While all things wax and nothing wanes
In lengthening daylight hours.
Across the hyacinth beds
The wind lags warm and sweet,
Across the hawthorn tops,
Across the blades of wheat …

Christina Rossetti (1830–1894) 'The Year's Windfalls'

The next morning, when Thomasin withdrew the curtains of her bedroom window, there stood the Maypole in the middle of the green, its top cutting into the sky. It had sprung up in the night, or rather early morning, like Jack's beanstalk. She opened the casement to get a better view of the garlands and posies that adorned it. The sweet perfume of the flowers had already spread into the surrounding air, which, being free from every taint, conducted to her lips a full measure of the fragrance received from the spire of blossom in its midst. At the top of the pole were crossed hoops decked with small flowers; beneath these came a milk-white zone of Maybloom; then a zone of bluebells, then of cowslips, then of lilacs, then of ragged-robins, daffodils, and so on, till the lowest stage was reached.

Thomas Hardy *The Return of the Native* (1878)

Newly dressed in the crystal of the rain the landscape recalls the earlier spring; the flowers of white wood-sorrel, the pink and white anemone and cuckoo flower, the thick-clustered, long stalked primroses and darker cowslips with their scentless sweetness pure as an infant's breath; the solitary wild cherry trees flowering among still leafless beech; the blackbirds of twilight and the flower-faced owls; the peewits wheeling after dusk; the jonquil and daffodil and arabis and leopard's bane of cottage gardens; the white clouds plunged in blue floating over the brown woods of the hills; the delicate thrushes with speckled breasts paler than their backs, motionless on dewy turf; and all the joys of life that come through the nostrils from the dark, not understood world which is unbolted for us by the delicate and savage fragrances of leaf and flower and grass and clod, of the plumage of birds and fur of animals …

Edward Thomas *The South Country* (1909)

She had been in that garden before, but never in May, with the apple blossom out and the wallflowers filling the air with their fragrance.

Flora Thompson *Candleford Green* (1943)

In spring on a warm day, if you sit in the lee of flowering quinces, you become quietly aware of a narcissus scent on the puffs of breeze … The furling twist of the bud, pink and white, opens into a globe of pale pink, ruffed with leaves – its mildness goes unnoticed if you walk by without stopping.

Jane Grigson *Fruit Book* (1980)

I went out into the garden in the morning dusk,
When sorrow enveloped me like a cloud;
And the breeze brought to my nostril the odour of spices,
As balm of healing for a sick soul.

Moses Ibn Ezra (1060–1138)

The Conval-lily is esteemed to have of all others, the sweetest and most agreeable perfume; not offensive or overbearing, even to those who are made uneasy with the perfumes of other sweet-scented flowers.

John Lawrence *The Flower Garden* (1726)

I cannot see what flowers are at my feet,
Nor what soft incense hangs upon the boughs,
But, in embalmed darkness, guess each sweet
Wherewith the seasonable month endows
The grass, the thicket, and the fruit-tree wild;
White hawthorn, and the pastoral eglantine;
Fast fading violets cover'd up in leaves;
And mid-May's eldest child,
The coming musk-rose, full of dewy wine,
The murmurous haunt of flies on summer eves.

John Keats 'Ode to a Nightingale' (1819)

Miranda! mark where shrinking from the gale,
Its silken leaves yet moist with early dew,
That fair faint flower, the Lily of the vale
Droops its meek head, and looks, methinks, like you!
Wrapp'd in a shadowy veil of tender green,
Its snowy bells a soft perfume dispense,
And bending as reluctant to be seen,
In simple loveliness it sooths the sense.
With bosom bared to meet the garish day,
The glaring Tulip, gaudy, undismay'd,
Offends the eye of taste; that turns away
To seek the Lily in her fragrant shade.
With such unconscious beauty, pensive, mild,
Miranda charms – Nature's soft modest child.

Charlotte Smith (1749–1806) Sonnet LX: 'To an Amiable Girl'

I'm sitting writing to you in a glade under a pine tree. There are quantities of little squat yellow bushes of a kind of broom everywhere that give a sweet scent and are the humming houses of bees.

Katherine Mansfield *Letters* (to Dorothy Brett, 22nd June 1922)

He waited for the morn to take that path and flow towards him. He could feel it coming in a warm breeze, so faint at first that it barely brushed across his skin, but rising little by little, and growing ever brisker till he was thrilled all over. He could also taste it coming with a more and more pronounced savour, bringing the healthful acridity of the open air, holding to his lips a feast of sugary aromatics, sour fruits, and milky shoots. Further, he could smell it coming with the perfumes which it culled upon its way – the scent of earth, the scent of the shady woods, the scent of the warm plants, the scent of living animals, a whole posy of scents, powerful enough to bring on dizziness.

Émile Zola *La Faute de l'Abbé Mouret* (1875)

The hill pines were sighing,
O'ercast and chill was the day:
A mist in the valley lying
Blotted the pleasant May.

But deep in the glen's bosom
Summer slept in the fire
Of the odorous gorse-blossom
And the hot scent of the brier.

A ribald cuckoo clamoured,
And out of the copse the stroke
Of the iron axe that hammered
The iron heart of the oak.

Anon a sound appalling,
As a hundred years of pride
Crashed, in the silence falling:
And the shadowy pine-trees sighed.

Robert Bridges Untitled (From *Short Poems*, 1894)

Syringahood
June

Horace Walpole described the fragrant 'Syringahood' of the third week in June when philadelphus (formerly called syringa – and confusingly so, since this is the Latin name for lilacs) bushes flower '… The flowers are white, and have a strong scent, which at some distance resembles Orange-flowers, but when near is too powerful for most persons'. And, later, he wrote to Lady Ossory, 'my house is a bower of tuberoses'. In the cold June of 1777 we learn of the 'dripping shrubberies … the summer has made a fausse-couche [miscarriage] too; I have no fruit; no flowers; no thrushes; no blackbirds.'

Tuberoses and philadelphus (mock orange) come in what perfumers call the 'heavy group' of scents, that contain the organic compound skatole, principal ingredient of civet, one of the perfumers' alchemistic loadstones until the civet cat became endangered. Skatole as its name suggests is a caca smell, repugnant for good reason, but curiously its beauty and magic are all in the dilution. On the air or in extreme dilution in plant flower alchemy it can be compulsive and heady to those that like it, and it can be found in jonquils, narcissi, viburnum, day lilies, tuberoses, honeysuckle, lilac and my favourite of all, *Philadelphus coronarius*.

Reading Walpole was the moment when I seriously questioned whether they had finer perceptions back then; or was it that things smelled more? Was it that scents travelled more easily in the incomparably clean air before the coming of the industrial revolution? An airy world, foul and felicitous smelling, which we cannot begin to imagine today. But we can read about. Reading all these fleeting mentions and dreamy interpretations of smell, it seems clear, to me at any rate, that the air was glossier and brighter with smell. Clear that, in an admittedly rural society, from the time before Shakespeare up until some point after the Great War it was taken as understood that every reader would be instantly and intimately familiar with the smell of wildflowers: primroses; violets; cowslips; lilac; lily of the valley; hawthorn; lime and fruit tree blossom; mock orange.

Horace's letters to George Montagu are highly engaging and illuminate the man and his private preoccupations, the smells of acacias, syringas, new cut hay, fireworks, lilac.

> I have just come out of the garden, the most oriental of evenings, and from breathing the odours beyond those of Araby. The Acacias, which the Arabians have sense to worship, are covered with blossoms, the honeysuckles dangle from every tree in festoons, the syringas are thickets of sweets, and the new cut hay of the field in the garden tempers the balmy gales with simple freshness, while a thousand sky rockets, launched into the air at Ranelagh or Marylebone, illuminate the scene and have an air of Haroun Alrachid's paradise.

The profoundly central notion of paradise and its biblical middle eastern roots was still the *sine qua non* of the garden. The scents of Strawberry Hill and the planting of the grove and shrubbery have been interpreted largely from these letters: roses, jasmine, honeysuckle, myrtle, lavender – the usual gamut of scented plants then available, plus pinks and clove carnations along with spring bulbs such as jonquils and hyacinths.

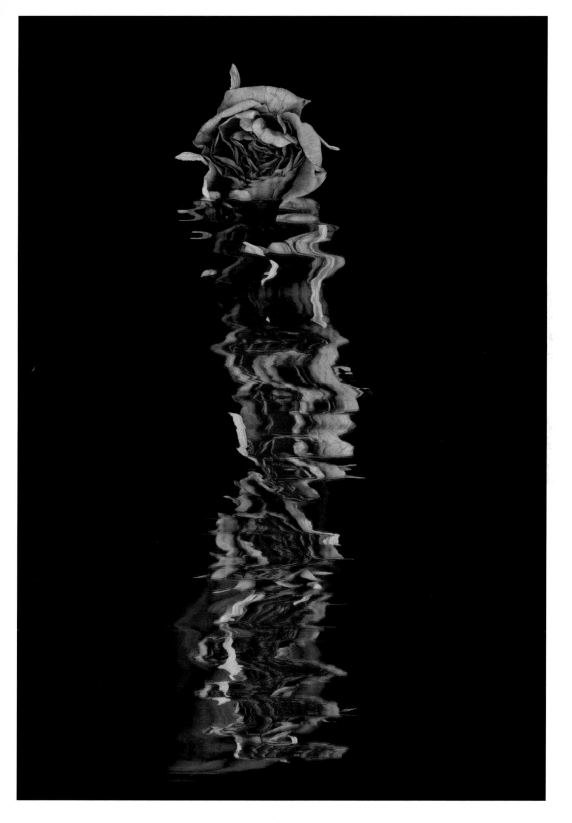

I smell the scent
Of the orange-flowers that wait
Till the fifth month to bloom …

Anon. Japanese from Heian period (794–1185)

That last week the syringa came out at San Salvatore, and all the acacias flowered.
No one had noticed how many acacias there were till one day the garden was full of
a new scent, and there were the delicate trees, the lovely successors to the wisteria,
hung all over among their trembling leaves with blossom. To lie under an acacia tree
that last week and look up through the branches at its frail leaves and white flowers
quivering against the blue of the sky, while the least movement of the air shook
down their scent, was a great happiness … When … everybody went away, even
after they had got to the bottom of the hill and passed through the iron gates into the
village they still could smell the acacias.

Elizabeth von Arnim *The Enchanted April* (1922)

A man ought to carry himself in the world as an orange tree would if it could walk
up and down in the garden, swinging perfume from every little censer it holds up in
the air.

Henry Ward Beecher (1813–1887)

Emma, her eyes half-closed, breathed in with deep sighs the fresh wind that was
blowing. They did not speak, lost as they were in the rush of their reverie. The
tenderness of the old days came back to their hearts, full and silent as the flowing
river, with the softness of the perfume of the syringas, and threw across their
memories shadows more immense and more sombre than those of the still willows
that lengthened out over the grass.

Gustave Flaubert *Madame Bovary* (1856)

The syringa, which had been a cloud of frozen air in the early morning light, hung
white and gold in the sun's warmth, lolling, showering scent and golden powder
from its open bosom.

Mollie Panter-Downes *One Fine Day* (1947)

That evening was the evening of the full moon. The garden was an enchanted place where all the flowers seemed white. The lilies … the orange-blossom, the white stocks, the white pinks, the white roses – you could see these as plainly as in the day-time …

Elizabeth von Arnim *The Enchanted April* (1922)

Emma would breathe the scent of its lining [the Viscount's cigar case], a mixture of tobacco and verbena.

Flaubert *Madame Bovary* (1856)

Ah, these jasmines, these white jasmines!
I seem to remember the first day when I filled my hands with
these jasmines, these white jasmines.
I have loved the sunlight, the sky and the green earth;
I have heard the liquid murmur of the river through the
darkness of midnight;
Autumn sunsets have come to me at the bend of a road in the
lonely waste, like a bride raising her veil to accept her lover.
Yet my memory is still sweet with the first white jasmines
that I held in my hands when I was a child.
Many a glad day has come in my life, and I have laughed with
merrymakers on festival nights.
On grey mornings of rain I have crooned many an idle song.
I have worn round my neck the evening wreath of bakulas woven
by the hand of love.
Yet my heart is sweet with the memory of the first fresh
jasmines that filled my hands when I was a child.

Rabindranath Tagore (1861–1941) 'The First Jasmines'

She and Stephen were in that stage of courtship which makes the most exquisite moment of youth, the freshest blossom-time of passion, – when each is sure of the other's love, but no formal declaration has been made, and all is mutual divination, exalting the most trivial word, the lightest gesture, into thrills delicate and delicious as wafted jasmine scent. The explicitness of an engagement wears off this finest edge of susceptibility; it is jasmine gathered and presented in a large bouquet.

George Eliot *The Mill on the Floss* (1860)

The back of the house [was] covered with jasmine, all in white flower, and smelling like a bottle of the most expensive perfume that is ever given for a birthday present.

E. Nesbit *Five Children and It* (1902)

I plucked a honeysuckle where
The hedge on high is quick with thorn,
And climbing for the prize, was torn,
And fouled my feet in quag-water;
And by the thorns and by the wind
The blossom that I took was thinn'd,
And yet I found it sweet and fair.
Thence to a richer growth I came,
Where, nursed in mellow intercourse,
The honeysuckles sprang by scores,
Not harried like my single stem,
All virgin lamps of scent and dew.
So from my hand that first I threw,
Yet plucked not any more of them.

Dante Gabriel Rossetti (1828–1882) 'The Honeysuckle'

The wind, one brilliant day, called
To my soul with a smell of jasmine.

'In return for the scent of my jasmine,
I'd like all the scent of your roses.'

'I have no roses; all the flowers
In my garden are dead.'

'Well then, I'll take the waters of the fountains
And the withered petals and the yellow leaves.'

The wind left. My heart was bleeding. And I said to myself:
'What have you done with the garden that was entrusted to you?'

Antonio Machado (1875–1939) 'The Wind, One Brilliant Day'

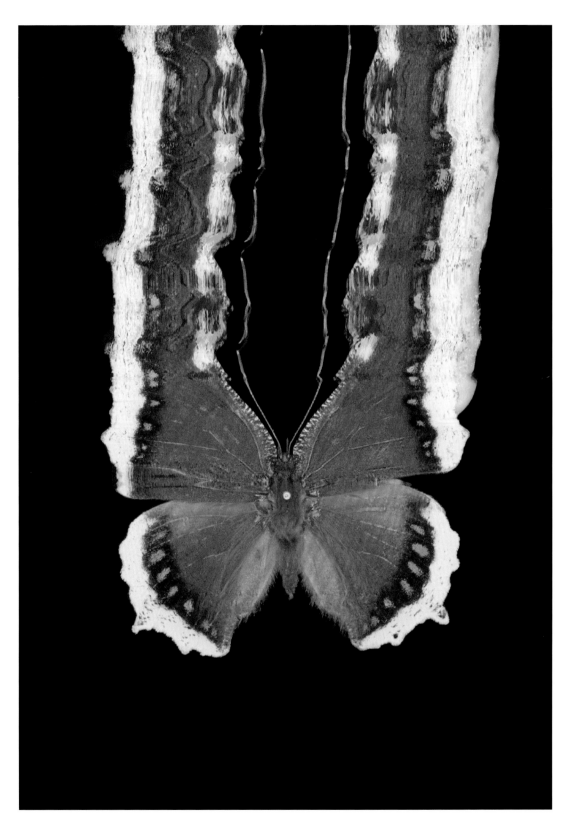

Hay, Grass, Coumarin
July

Coumarin is an organic volatile associated with the smell of new-mown hay. The name comes from a French term for the tonka bean, *coumarou*, one of the sources from which coumarin was first isolated as a natural product in 1820. Celia Lyttelton in her book *The Scent Trail* says that you really do want to lie down as a sleepiness steals over you when you stand in a tonka-bean field and inhale it. That sweet odour has been used in perfumes since 1882. Sweet woodruff and sweet clover also have this smell and were used for 'strewing' in mediaeval houses owing to their high coumarin content. When it occurs in high concentrations in forage plants, coumarin is somewhat bitter-tasting and is therefore presumed to be produced by plants as a defence chemical against predation. Strangely both the synthesised and natural coumarin are powerful anticoagulants, vitamin K antagonists, used in rodenticides like warfarin. But the dilute smell on the air is a huge bringer of a sense of plenitude and insouciance.

And when the *Poets* would describe the utmost delight of the touch, they present us with a Prospect of the *Golden Age*, when the whole world was but one Garden, in which we see the tendernesse of the Grasse & flowry bankes invites every body to lye downe, and enjoy the easiness of those soft and fragrant beds … to vanquish & captivate all the rest of the senses.

John Evelyn, in the seventeenth century, has a vision of *Elysium Brittanicum* very much predicated on the lost Eden that all the troubles of that century, the millenarians and praise-god-barebones were hoping to find in heaven and on earth. But the smell of newly mown hay has always been a tonic. Martial, perhaps the most obviously sensual of Roman poets and famous for epigrams which are short, witty and nostalgic for his birthplace in Hispania, captures smell with extraordinary sharpness. He has the usual – curious to modern minds – reference to sheep-cropped grass, although this is the ancient form of 'mowing', describing his mistress kissing him 'as she bites an apple', her breath smelling 'as of grass which a sheep has just cropped … of myrtle … spice gatherer … rubbed amber … a fire made pale, of the earth lightly sprinkled with summer rain.'

Horace Walpole, writing in old age, argued that sound and scent are (unlike the 'picturing practices', which is how he referred to the gardens of Brown and Kent) the vital signs of a gardening life. His longing is to smell mown grass in a lawn 'green enough to disgust a Frenchman'. And clearly his ambivalence towards foreigners remained with him to the end. 'I was not quite so content by daylight; some foreigners dined here and though they admired our verdure, it mortified me by its brownness; we have not had drop of rain this month to cool the tip of the daisies.' Lawns were more meadows than the machinecut patches of today, but about the same time Rousseau wrote in *Julie, or the New Héloïse* about the smell of lawn in an orchard, '… the verdant turf, thick, but short and close, was intermixed with wild thyme, balm, sweet marjoram, and other scented herbs'. In the last century Philip Larkin, not the first poet to spring to mind as pastoral, but always astonishing in observation, wrote of 'Cut Grass' in 1971

Cut grass lies frail:
Brief is the breath
Mown stalks exhale.
Long, long the death …

He had not been awake more than ten minutes when he heard feet running along the corridor and Mary was at the door. The next minute she was in the room and had run across to his bed, bringing with her a waft of fresh air full of the scent of the morning. 'You've been out! You've been out! There's that nice smell of leaves!' he cried.

Frances Hodgson Burnett *The Secret Garden* (1911)

It is not only leaves you smell when you stand under the trees today; you smell the black wet boughs and stems, the 'forest' smell … Do you know the smell of wet sand? Does it make you think of going down to the beach in the evening light after a rainy day and gathering the damp drift wood (it will dry on top of the stove) and picking up for a moment the long branches of sea weed that the waves have tossed and listening to the gulls who stand reflcted in the gleaming sand …

Katherine Mansfield *Letters* (to S. S. Koteliansky, 17th May 1915)

The strawberries exhaled a sweet perfume – a perfume of youth – especially those little ones which are gathered in the woods, and which are far more aromatic than the large ones grown in gardens, for these breathe an insipid odour suggestive of the watering-pot.

Émile Zola *Le Ventre de Paris* (1873)

It was a stagnant, warm, and misty night, full of all the heavy perfumes of new vegetation not yet dried by hot sun, and among these particularly the scent of the fern.

Thomas Hardy *The Return of the Native* (1878)

The season developed and matured. Another year's instalment of flowers, leaves, nightingales, thrushes, finches, and such ephemeral creatures, took up their positions where only a year ago others had stood in their place when these were nothing more than germs and inorganic particles. Rays from the sunrise drew forth the buds and stretched them into long stalks, lifted up sap in noiseless streams, opened petals, and sucked out scents in invisible jets and breathings.

Thomas Hardy *Tess of the d'Urbervilles* (1821)

Love, meet me in the green glen,
Beside the tall elm-tree,
Where the sweetbrier smells so sweet agen;
There come with me,
Meet me in the green glen.

Meet me at the sunset
Down in the green glen,
Where we've often met
By hawthorn-tree and foxes' den,
Meet me in the green glen.

Meet me in the green glen,
By sweetbrier bushes there;
Meet me by your own sen,
Where the wild thyme blossoms fair.
Meet me in the green glen.

Meet me by the sweetbrier,
By the molehill swelling there;
Where the west glows like a fire
God's crimson bed is there.
Meet me in the green glen.

John Clare 'Love in the Green Glen' (*c.*1850)

Myrrah loved her father, but not as a daughter should,
and then was hidden by the covering bark:
oozing those tears, that pour from the tree as fragrance,
and whose droplets take their name from the girl.

Ovid *Ars Amatoria* (2nd century AD)

The new-mown hay that scents the swelling breeze,
Or cottage-chimney smoking through the trees …

Gilbert White 'Evening at Selbourne' (1789)

I have been here before,
But when or how I cannot tell:
I know the grass beyond the door,
The sweet keen smell,
The sighing sound, the lights around the shore.

Dante Gabriel Rossetti 'Sudden Light' (1863)

The verdant turf, thick, but short and close, was intermixed with wild thyme,
balm, sweet marjoram, and other fragrant herbs. You might perceive a thousand
wildflowers dazzle our eyes …

Rousseau *La Nouvelle Héloïse* (1761)

His voice had the faint, infinitely sweet twang of certain Irishry; a thing as delicate and
intangible as the scent of lime flowers.

Joseph Conrad and Ford Maddox Ford *Romance* (1903)

Lime Flowers and Tea Thereof

June is the time for lime blossom in Europe and for tisanes made from the lime tree – linden or *tilleul* – slightly astringent because of a high tannin content. Linden is the tea into which Proust dunks the celebrated madeleine. *Tilia cordata*, also known as small-leaved lime, is considered the most potent species from which a herbal infusion of flowers, leaves and bark are boiled and steeped; these have been used in folk medicine across cultures to relieve high blood pressure, calm anxiety and soothe digestion. The heady, toxic, slightly weeping silver lime, *Tilia tomentosa*, flowers in July in England. This is when I like to lie beneath this ball gown of a tree with the drunken bees and think of Isak Dinesen on lime blossom 'The Lime trees were in flower. But in the early morning only a faint scent drifted through the garden, an airy message, an aromatic echo of the dreams during the short summer night.'

The tea smell is so important to me in my garden, always stopping for tea and a cigarette. Tea and tea-time so integral to gardening life. Henry James loved afternoons ('Summer afternoon – summer afternoon; to me those have always been the two most beautiful words in the English language.') and tea-times: 'There are few hours in life more agreeable than the hour dedicated to the ceremony known as afternoon tea.' P.G. Woodhouse is good at this cosy ritual also. 'The cup of tea on arrival at a country house is a thing which, as a rule, I particularly enjoy. I like the crackling logs, the shaded lights, the scent of buttered toast, the general atmosphere of leisured cosiness.' Tea goes along with the joy of pottering, or snailing if you are Lord Emsworth: 'For perhaps an hour, til the day had cooled off a little, he would read his Pig book in the Library. After he would go and take a sniff at a rose or two and possibly do a bit of snailing. These mild pleasures were all his simple soul demanded.' Almost the antithesis, yet grasping at the same thing, is Osbert Sitwell on Italian gardens. 'I think no English garden is as lovely as a foreign one. These gardens are created for rest in cool surroundings, for idleness and sauntering and imaginative thought … but never for a show of tinkling tea-cups and hoarse cries of "Love-all".'

I thought of Italian gardens when I was making a garden at our new house – specifically that of Don Fabrizio Corbera, Prince of Salina, in *The Leopard*. I think subconsciously I remembered the extraordinarily vivid passages where the Prince thinks of his garden as 'a garden for the blind', though I winced at the Count's description of his faded former lovers, now 'rich in daughters in law'.

Air swept lindens yield
Their scent and rustle down their perfumed showers
Of bloom …

Matthew Arnold (1822–1888) 'The Scholar-Gipsy'

Between two golden tufts of summer grass,
I see the world through hot air as through glass,
And by my face sweet lights and colours pass.

Before me, dark against the fading sky,
I watch three mowers mowing, as I lie:
With brawny arms they sweep in harmony …

The music of the scythes that glide and leap,
The young men whistling as their great arms sweep,
And all the perfume and sweet sense of sleep,

The weary butterflies that droop their wings,
The dreamy nightingale that hardly sings,
And all the lassitude of happy things,

Are mingling with the warm and pulsing blood
That gushes through my veins a languid flood,
And feeds my spirit as the sap a bud.

Edmund Gosse 'Lying in the Grass' (1873)

There had never been such a June in Eagle Country. Usually, it was a month of moods, with abrupt alternations of belated frost and midsummer heat; this year, day followed day in a sequence of temperate beauty. Every morning a breeze blew steadily from the hills. Toward noon it built up great canopies of white cloud that threw a cool shadow over fields and woods; then before sunset the clouds dissolved again, and the western light raining its unobstructed brightness on the valley.

   On such an afternoon Charity Royall lay on the ridge above a sunlit valley, her face pressed to the earth and the warm currents of the grass running through her. Directly in her line of vision a blackberry branch laid its frail white flowers and blue-green leaves against the sky. Just beyond, a tuft of sweet-fern uncurled between the beaded shoots of the grass, and a small yellow butterfly vibrated over them like a fleck of sunshine. This was all she saw; but she felt, above her and about her, the strong growth of the beeches clothing the ridge, the rounding of pale green cones on countless spruce branches, the push of myriads of sweet-fern fronds in the cracks of the stony slope below the wood, and the crowding shoots of meadowsweet and yellow flags in the pasture beyond. All this bubbling of sap and slipping of sheathes and bursting of calyxes was carried to her on mingled currents of fragrance. Every leaf and bud and blade seemed to contribute its exhalation to the pervading sweetness in which the pungency of pine-sap prevailed over the spice of thyme and the subtle perfume of fern, and all were merged in a moist earth-smell that was like the breath of some huge sun-warmed animal.

Edith Wharton *Summer* (1917)

Plants were growing in thick disorder on the reddish clay, flowers sprouted in all directions, and the myrtle hedges seemed put there to prevent movement rather than guide it. At the end a statue of Flora speckled with yellow-black lichen exhibited her centuries-old charms with an air of resignation; on each side were benches holding quilted cushions, also of grey marble; and in a corner the gold of an acacia tree introduced a sudden note of gaiety. Every sod seemed to exude a yearning for beauty soon muted by languor.

But the garden, hemmed and almost squashed between these barriers, was exhaling scents that were cloying, fleshy and slightly putrid, like the aromatic liquids distilled from the relics of certain saints; the carnations superimposed their pungence on the formal fragrance of roses and the oily emanations of magnolias drooping in corners; and somewhere beneath it all was a faint smell of mint mingling with a nursery whiff of acacia and the jammy one of myrtle; from a grove beyond the wall came an erotic waft of early orange blossom.

It was a garden for the blind: a constant offence to the eyes, a pleasure strong if somewhat crude to the nose. The Paul Neyron roses, whose cuttings he had himself bought in Paris, had degenerated; first stimulated and then enfeebled by the strong if languid pull of Sicilian earth … distilling a dense almost indecent scent which no French horticulturist would have dared hope for. The Prince put one under his nose and seemed to be sniffing the thigh of a dancer from the Opera. Bendicò, to whom it was also proffered, drew back in disgust and hurried off in search of healthier sensations amid dead lizards and manure.

Giuseppe Tomasi di Lampedusa *The Leopard* (1958)

Luscious Sweet
August

Virginia Woolf wrote 'love is chiefly smell'. High summer is chiefly smell and sex also. In literature it seems to be the erotically charged expression of the garden, an enticement, a temptation, such as Gerald Durrell felt in a magnolia whose 'thick, sweet scent hung over the veranda languorously, the scent that was an enchantment luring you out into the mysterious, moonlit countryside'. The innocence of lusty May when the first and more dainty roses show, is superseded by gradually more exotic and intoxicating scents, more pillowed and ruffled roses. Hot weather finally comes, and heat is very potent and emotionally exciting. The smell map of late summer begins to tip into decay, hinting at rot and regret. But not yet. The warm nights welcome the scents of *Datura* and star jasmine. The attar, or essential oil, of jasmine consists principally of benzyl acetate and allied benzyls along with indole, which cannot be synthesised satisfactorily, and which gives a sweet sultry intoxicating nuance to jasmine, lilac, tuberose, orange flowers. This grouping is never found in leaves and is typical of many heavy-scented flowers, lightened in the case of jasmine by certain fruit-scented substances giving a very exquisite-natured smell which we encounter in lily of the valley, but further, and the scent of jasmine is long, because of balsamic substances that give it a peculiar richness and warmth. I like to have bowls of roses on my desk. Roses contain none of the muddling indole. The alchemy of nature, and especially of the smell of roses is in the complex layering of ingredients, often at infinitesimal levels, the intricacy of which is impossible to imitate and is crucial and decisive in the character for the entire complex. Alcohols predominate in the rose group of smells and geraniol often, but natural selection operates to produce a very specificity to the rose scent by assembling substances such as phenethyl alcohol in layers. The smell of a particular rose may be laden with fruit-scented substances as in Hybrid Teas or Noisettes; or laden with clove spiciness as in *Rosa brunonii*, the Himalayan musk rose – hence the name. When Colette writes of roses, it is the '… splendour, a conspiracy of perfumes, petalous flesh that tempts the nose, the lips, the teeth … It is riper than fruit, more sensual than cheek or breast'. She is very specific about her rose scents '… roses the colour of nasturtiums, with a scent of peaches; starved looking roses tinged with dirty mauve that smelled of crushed ants; orange roses that smelled of nothing at all; and finally a little horror of a rosebush with tiny yellowish flowers covered in hairs, badly set on their stalks, bushing out all over the place, and giving off an odour like a musk-filled menagerie, like a gymnasium frequented exclusively by young red-headed women, like artificial vanilla extract.'

The seeds Dickon and Mary had planted grew as if fairies had tended them. Satiny poppies of all tints danced in the breeze by the score, gaily defying flowers which had lived in the garden for years and which it might be confessed seemed rather to wonder how such new people had got there. And the roses – the roses! Rising out of the grass, tangled around the sundial, wreathing the tree trunks, and hanging from their branches, climbing up the walls and spreading over them with long garlands falling in cascades – they came alive day by day, hour by hour. Fair fresh leaves, and buds – and buds – tiny at first but swelling and working magic until they burst and uncurled into cups of scent delicately spilling themselves over their brims and filling the garden air.

Colin saw it all, watching each change as it took place. Every morning he was brought out and every hour of each day when it did not rain, he spent in the garden. Even grey days pleased him. He would lie on the grass 'watching things growing,' he said. If you watched long enough, he declared, you could see buds unsheathe themselves. Also, you could make the acquaintance of strange busy insect things running about on various unknown but evidently serious errands, sometimes carrying tiny scraps of straw or feather or food or climbing blades of grass as if they were trees from whose tops one could look out and explore the country. A mole throwing up its mound at the end of its burrow and making its way out at last with the long-nailed paws and which looked so like elfish hands, had absorbed him one whole morning.

Frances Hodgson Burnett *The Secret Garden* (1911)

Where rustic taste at leisure trimly weaves
The rose and straggling woodbine to the eaves,–
And on the crowded spot that pales enclose
The white and scarlet daisy rears in rows,–
Training the trailing peas in bunches neat,
Perfuming evening with a luscious sweet,–

John Clare 'Rural Evening' (1821)

It was a perfect spot for the middle period of a Sunday in June, and its felicity seemed to come partly from an antique sun-dial which, rising in front of us and forming the centre of a small intricate parterre, measured the moments ever so slowly and made them safe for leisure and talk. The garden bloomed in the suffused afternoon, the tall beeches stood still for an example, and, behind and above us, a rose-tree of many seasons, clinging to the faded grain of the brick, expressed the whole character of the scene in a familiar exquisite smell.

Henry James 'The Author of Beltraffio' (1884)

I think I am quite wicked with roses; I like to gather them and smell them till they have no scent left.

George Eliot *The Mill on the Floss* (1860)

The very rose-trees, at which Adam stopped to pluck one, looked as if they grew wild; they were all huddled together in bushy masses, now flaunting with wide open petals, almost all of them of the streaked pink-and-white kind, which doubtless dated from the union of the houses of York and Lancaster. Adam was wise enough to choose a compact Provence rose that peeped out half-smothered by its flaunting scentless neighbours, and held it in his hand – he thought he should be more at ease holding something in his hand – as he walked on to the far end of the garden …

George Eliot *Adam Bede* (1859)

Beyond his hope, Eve separate he spies,
Veild in a Cloud of Fragrance, where she stood,
Half spi'd, so thick the Roses bushing round
About her glowd, oft stooping to support
Each Flour of slender stalk, whose head though gay
Carnation, Purple, Azure, or spect with Gold,
Hung drooping unsustaind, them she upstaies
Gently with Mirtle band, mindless the while,
Her self, though fairest unsupported Flour,
From her best prop so farr, and storm so nigh.

John Milton *Paradise Lost* (1667)

And the woodbine spices are wafted abroad,
And the musk of the rose is blown …

Alfred, Lord Tennyson 'Maud' (1855)

For them the sun shines ever in full might
Throughout our earthly night;
There, reddening with the rose, their paradise,
A fair green pleasance, lies,
Cool beneath shade of incense-bearing trees,
And rich with golden fruit …
Over the lovely region everywhere
Fragrance in the air …

Pindar (518–438 BC) *Threnos VII*, trans. Walter Headlam

I said: This is a beautiful fresh rose.
I said: I will delight me with its scent,
Will watch its lovely curve of languishment,
Will watch its leaves unclose, its hearth unclose …

Christina Rossetti (1830–1894) 'Once for All'

I sing of Brooks, of Blossomes, Birds and Bowers:
Of April, May, of June, and July-Flowers.
I sing of May-poles, Hock-carts, Wassails, Wakes,
Of Bride-grooms, Brides, and of their Bridall-cakes.
I write of Youth, of Love, and have Accesse
By these, to sing of cleanly Wantonesse.
I sing of Dewes, of Raines, and piece by piece
Of Balme, of Oyle, of Spice and Amber-Greece.
I sing of Times trans-shifting; and I write
How Roses first came Red, and Lilies White.
I write of Groves, of Twilights, and I sing
The Court of Mab, and of the Fairie-King …

Robert Herrick 'Hesperides' (1648)

Enobarbus: I will tell you.
The barge she sat in, like a burnish'd throne,
Burned on the water: the poop was beaten gold;
Purple the sails, and so perfumed that
The winds were lovesick with them; the oars were silver,
Which to the tune of flutes kept stroke, and made
The water which they beat to follow faster,
As amorous of their strokes. For her own person,
It beggar'd all description: she did lie
In her pavilion, cloth-of-gold of tissue,
O'erpicturing that Venus where we see
The fancy outwork nature: on each side her
Stood pretty dimpled boys, like smiling Cupids,
With divers-colour'd fans, whose wind did seem
To glow the delicate cheeks which they did cool,
And what they undid did.

Agrippa: O, rare for Antony.

Enobarbus: Her gentlewomen, like the Nereides,
So many mermaids, tended her i' th' eyes,
And made their bends adornings. At the helm
A seeming mermaid steers: the silken tackle
Swell with the touches of those flower-soft hands
That yarely frame the office. From the barge
A strange invisible perfume hits the sense
Of the adjacent wharfs. The city cast
Her people out upon her; and Antony,
Enthroned i' th' marketplace, did sit alone,
Whistling to th' air; which, but for vacancy,
Had gone to gaze on Cleopatra too,
And made a gap in nature.

Agrippa: Rare Egyptian!

William Shakespeare *Anthony and Cleopatra* (1607)

My sensations are all glossy, spruce, voluptuous, and fine: they wear a candied coat, and are in holiday trim. I see the beds of … tall hollyhocks and the broad sunflowers, caked in gold, with bees buzzing round them; wildernesses of pinks, and hot-glowing peonies; poppies run to seed; the sugared lily; and faint mignonette, all ranged in order, and as thick as they can grow.

William Hazlitt 'Why Distant Objects Please' (1882)

Here comes the time when vibrating on its stem each flower diffuses like a censer; the sounds and the fragrances turn in the evening's air; melancholy waltz and languorous vertigo!

Baudelaire *Les Fleurs du Mal* (1857)

Soon will the musk-carnations break and swell,
Soon shall we have gold-dusted snapdragon,
Sweet William with its homely cottage smell,
And stocks in fragrant blow;
Roses that down the alleys shine afar,
 And open, jasmine muffled lattices,
And groups under the dreaming garden trees,
And the full moon, and the white evening-star.

Matthew Arnold 'Thyrsis' (1856)

The hedge allowed us a glimpse, inside the park, of an alley bordered with jasmine, pansies, and verbenas, among which the stocks held open their fresh plump purses, of a pink as fragrant and as faded as old Spanish leather, while on the gravel-path a long watering-pipe, painted green, coiling across the ground, poured, where its holes were, over the flowers whose perfume those holes inhaled, a vertical and prismatic fan of infinitesimal, rainbow-coloured drops. Suddenly I stood still, unable to move, as happens when something appears that requires not only our eyes to take it in, but involves a deeper kind of perception and takes possession of the whole of our being.

Marcel Proust *Swann's Way* (1913)

Like Maia's son he stood
And shook his Plumes, that Heav'nly fragrance filld
The circuit wide. Strait knew him all the Bands
Of Angels under watch; and to his state,
And to his message high in honour rise;
For on Som message high they guessd him bound.
Their glittering Tents he passd, and now is come
Into the blissful field, through Groves of Myrrhe,
And flouring Odours, Cassia, Nard, and Balme;
A Wilderness of sweets; for Nature here
Wantond as in her prime, and plaid at will
Her Virgin Fancies, pouring forth more sweet,
Wilde above Rule or Art; enormous bliss.
Him through the spicie Forrest onward com
Adam discernd, as in the dore he sat
Of his coole Bowre, while now the mounted Sun
Shot down direct his fervid Raies, to warme
Earths inmost womb, more warmth then Adam needs;
And Eve within, due at her hour prepar'd
For dinner savourie fruits, of taste to please
True appetite, and not disrelish thirst
Of nectarous draughts between, from milkie stream,
Berrie or Grape: to whom thus Adam call'd.

Milton *Paradise Lost*: Book Five (1667)

Through the open door, stealthily, came the scent of madonna lilies, almost as if it were
prowling abroad … A half-moon, dusky gold, was sinking behind the black sycamore
at the end of the garden making the sky dull purple with its glow. Nearer, a dim white
fence of lilies went across the garden, and the air all round seemed to stir with scent as
if it were alive. He went across the beds of pinks, whose keen perfume came sharply
across the rocking, heavy scent of lilies, and stood alongside the white barrier of
flowers. They flagged all loose, as if they were panting. The scent made him drunk …
Behind him the great flowers leaned as if they were calling. And then, like a shock,
he caught another perfume, something raw and coarse. Hunting round, he found the
purple iris, touched their fleshy throats and their dark, grasping hands. At any rate, he
had found something. They stood stiff in the darkness. Their scent was brutal.

D. H. Lawrence *Sons and Lovers* (1913)

All trees and simples great and small,
That balmie leife do beir,
Nor thay were painted on a wall,
Na mair they move or steir …

The flurishes and fragrant flowres,
Throw Phoebus fostring heit,
Refresht with dew and silver showres,
Casts up ane odor sweit.

The clogged busie humming beis,
That never thinks to drowne,
On flowers and flourishes of treis,
Collects their liquor browne …

Alexander Hume (1558–1609) 'Of the Day Estivall'

I went apart into the orchard. No nook in the grounds more sheltered and more Eden-like; it was full of trees, it bloomed with flowers: a very high wall shut it out from the court, on one side; on the other, a beech avenue screened it from the lawn. At the bottom was a sunk fence; its sole separation from lonely fields: a winding walk, bordered with laurels and terminating in a giant horse-chestnut, circled at the base by a seat, led down to the fence. Here one could wander unseen. While such honey-dew fell, such silence reigned, such gloaming gathered, I felt as if I could haunt such shade for ever; but in threading the flower and fruit parterres at the upper part of the enclosure, enticed there by the light the now rising moon cast on this more open quarter, my step is stayed – not by sound, not by sight, but once more by a warning fragrance. Sweet-briar and southernwood, jasmine, pink, and rose have long been yielding their evening sacrifice of incense: this new scent is neither of shrub nor flower; it is – I know it well – it is Mr. Rochester's cigar. I look round and I listen. I see trees laden with ripening fruit. I hear a nightingale warbling in a wood half a mile off; no moving form is visible, no coming step audible; but that perfume increases: I must flee. I make for the wicket leading to the shrubbery, and I see Mr. Rochester entering. I step aside into the ivy recess; he will not stay long: he will soon return whence he came, and if I sit still he will never see me.

But no – eventide is as pleasant to him as to me, and this antique garden as attractive; and he strolls on, now lifting the gooseberry-tree branches to look at the fruit, large as plums, with which they are laden; now taking a ripe cherry from the wall; now stooping towards a knot of flowers, either to inhale their fragrance or to admire the dew-beads on their petals.

Charlotte Brontë *Jane Eyre* (1847)

A faint, sickening scent of irises
Persists all morning. Here in a jar on the table
A fine proud spike of purple irises
Rising above the class-room litter, makes me unable
To see the class's lifted and bended faces
Save in a broken pattern, amid purple and gold and sable.

I can smell the gorgeous bog-end, in its breathless
Dazzle of may-blobs, when the marigold glare overcast you
With fire on your cheeks and your brow and your chin as you dipped
Your face in the marigold bunch, to touch and contrast you,
Your own dark mouth with the bridal faint lady-smocks,
Dissolved on the golden sorcery you should not outlast …

You upon the dry, dead beech-leaves, in the fire of night
Burnt like a sacrifice; you invisible;
Only the fire of darkness, and the scent of you!
– And yes, thank God, it still is possible
The healing days shall close the darkness up
Wherein we fainted like a smoke or dew.

D. H. Lawrence (1885–1930) 'Scent of Irises'

Weed, moss-weed,
root tangled in sand,
sea-iris, brittle flower,
one petal like a shell
is broken,
and you print a shadow
like a thin twig.

Fortunate one,
scented and stinging,
rigid myrrh-bud,
camphor-flower,
sweet and salt – you are wind
in our nostrils."

H. D. 'Sea Iris' (from *Sea Garden*, 1916)

The summer's flower is to the summer sweet
Though to itself it only live and die,
But if that flower with base infection meet,
The basest weed outbraves his dignity:
For sweetest things turn sourest by their deeds;
Lilies that fester smell far worse than weeds.

William Shakespeare (1564–1616) Sonnet 94

[Dragon arum is] the most fiendish plant I know of, the sort of thing Beelzebub
might pluck to make a bouquet for his mother-in-law … it looks as if it had been
made out of a sow's ear for the spathe, and the tail of a rat that died of Elephantiasis
for the spadix. The whole thing is mingling of unwholesome greens, livid purples,
and pallid pinks, the livery of putrescence in fact, and it possesses an odour to match
the colouring.

E. A. Bowles *My Garden in Spring* (1914)

Have you seen but a bright lily grow,
Before rude hands have touch'd it?
Ha' you mark'd but the fall o' the snow
Before the soil hath smutch'd it?
Ha' you felt the wool o' the beaver?
Or swan's down ever?
Or have smelt o' the bud o' the briar?
Or the nard in the fire?
Or have tasted the bag of the bee?
Oh so white! Oh so soft! Oh so sweet is she!

Ben Jonson *A Celebration of Charis* (1640)

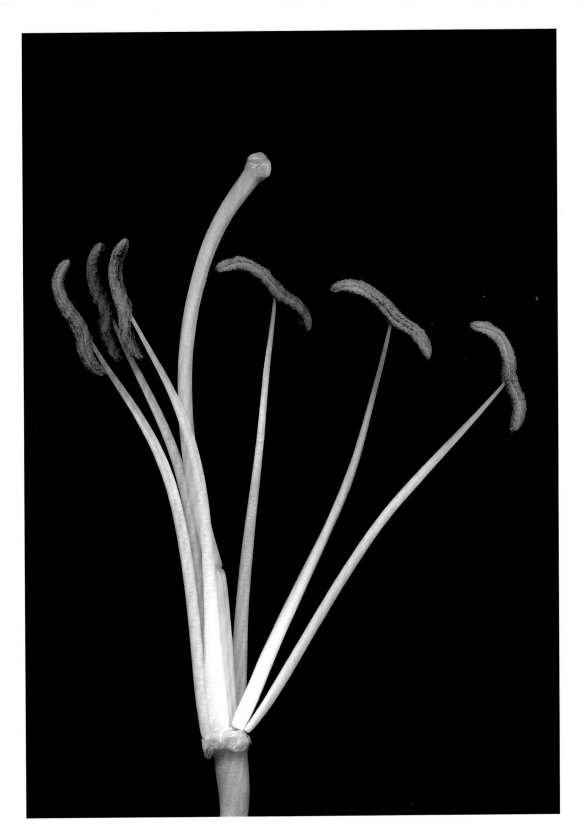

Bees

I was a beekeeper until repeated stingings made my body react badly and I had to give it up, very regrettably. It was a realm I had always warmed to. As a child I was fearless and found bees, bumblebees especially – even wasps and snakes – friendly, and I had a passion for frogs, newts and toads. The smell of apiary is what I remembered from the following passage by Tolstoy; but the mind plays tricks and going back to it I can find no direct reference to smell here now … but it makes you think of the smell of tea in the apiary, and he does mention the flowering lime trees, the smell of which makes bees almost drunk.

> Going along the narrow path to a little uncut meadow covered on one side with thick clumps of brilliant heart's-ease among which stood up here and there tall, dark green tufts of Hellebore … Levin settled his guests in the dense, cool shade of the young aspens on a bench and some stumps purposely put there for visitors to the bee house who might be afraid of the bees, and he went off himself to the hut to get bread, cucumbers, and fresh honey, to regale them with … It made his eyes giddy to watch the bees and drones whirling round and round about the same spot while among them the working bees flew in and out with spoils or in search of them, always in the same direction into the wood to the flowering lime trees and back to the hives.

Leo Tolstoy *Anna Karenina*, trans. 1901 Constance Garnett

Honey bees use smell in a number of ways both in the outside world and inside their colonies. Inside the hive, among the colony of sisters, scents depress the development of almost all the bees to make them worker bees, or to make them develop into drones and even to trigger and control the building of queen cells. Smells are also used among the sisters to signal homing and swarming. Smell is fast and efficient for signalling in a swarm. It engulfs the many moving individuals, whereas sound and sight are confused by massed numbers. Once again, the story is only just beginning to unravel – while at the same time the whole bee world is unravelling very fast as is clearly evident in colony collapse. Along with air pollution, heavy air-born particulates, neo-nicotinoids are creating an insect-less void, and one of the factors in this must be that we are disturbing the functions of smell, causing havoc and anarchy in this highly specialised and finely balanced world of which we know practically nothing. We are always, and understandably, focused upon the effects of air pollutants on us humans, almost oblivious of the terrifying storm of poison we have unleashed upon tiny, even microscopic, fragile flying things or fungi. The paucity of our imagination prevents us grasping this enormity.

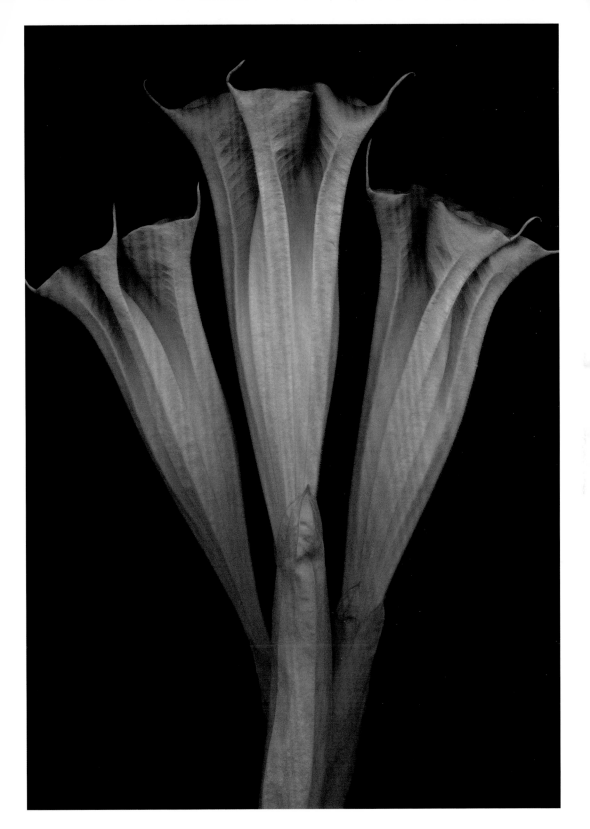

Every fine day, throughout the summer, she sat there 'watching the bees'. She was combining duty and pleasure, for, if they swarmed, she was making sure of not losing the swarm; and, if they did not, it was still, as she said, 'a trate' to sit there, feeling the warmth of the sun, smelling the flowers, and watching 'the craturs' go in and out of the hives.

Flora Thompson *Lark Rise* (1939)

Golden the hive, and yet 'tis true
Bees wrought it not from gold, but dew.

Macedonius (6th century AD) 'On A Mercenary Beauty', trans. Richard Garnett

First, for thy Bees a quiet Station find,
And lodge 'em under Covert of the Wind:
For Winds, when homeward they return, will drive
The loaded Carriers from their Ev'ning Hive.
Far from the Cows and Goats insulting Crew,
That trample down the Flow'rs, and brush the Dew …

But near a living Stream their Mansion place,
Edg'd round with Moss, and tufts of matted Grass:
And plant (the Winds impetuous rage to stop,)
Wild Olive Trees, or Palms, before the buisie Shop:
That when the youthful Prince, with loud allarm,
Calls out the vent'rous Colony to swarm;
When first their way thro' yielding Air they wing,
New to the Pleasures of their native Spring;
The Banks of Brooks may make a cool retreat
For the raw Souldiers from the scalding Heat:
And neighb'ring Trees, with friendly Shade invite
The Troops unus'd to long laborious Flight.
Then o'er the running Stream, or standing Lake,
A Passage for thy weary People make;
With Osier Floats the standing Water strow;
Of massy Stones make Bridges, if it flow:
That basking in the Sun thy Bees may lye,
And resting there, their flaggy Pinions dry:
When late returning home, the laden Host,
By raging Winds is wreck'd upon the Coast.

Wild Thyme and Sav'ry set around their Cell,
Sweet to the taste, and fragrant to the Smell:
Set rows of Rosemary with flow'ring Stem,
And let the purple Vi'lets drink the Stream

Sweet Gardens, full of Saffron Flow'rs, invite
The wandring Gluttons, and retard their Flight.
Besides, the God obscene, who frights away,
With his Lath Sword, the Thiefs and Birds of Prey.
With his own hand, the Guardian of the Bees,
For Slips of Pines, may search the Mountain Trees:
And with wild Thyme and Sav'ry, plant the Plain,
'Till his hard horny Fingers ake with Pain:
And deck with fruitful Trees the Fields around,
And with refreshing Waters drench the Ground.

Virgil *Georgics* Book IV (*c.*29 BC) trans. John Dryden

These I have loved:
White plates and cups, clean-gleaming,
Ringed with blue lines; and feathery, faery dust;
Wet roofs, beneath the lamplight; the strong crust
Of friendly bread; and many-tasting food;
Rainbows; and the blue bitter smoke of wood;
And radiant raindrops couching in cool flowers;
And flowers themselves, that sway through sunny hours,
Dreaming of moths that drink them under the moon …
The good smell of old clothes; and other such,
The comfortable smell of friendly fingers,
Hair's fragrance, and the musty reek that lingers
About dead leaves and last year's ferns …
Moist black earthen mould;
Sleep; and high places; footprints in the dew;
And oaks; and brown horse-chestnuts, glossy-new;
And new-peeled sticks …

Rupert Brooke 'The Great Lover' (1915)

Ah God! to see the branches stir
Across the moon at Grantchester!
To smell the thrilling-sweet and rotten
Unforgettable, unforgotten
River-smell, and hear the breeze
Sobbing in the little trees.

Rupert Brooke 'The Old Vicarage, Grantchester' (1912)

July:
Heavy is the green of the fields, heavy the trees
With foliage hang, drowsy the hum of bees
In the thund'rous air: the crowded scents lie low
Thro' tangle of weeds the river runneth slow.

Robert Bridges 'Eclogue I: The Months' (From *New Poems*, 1899)

I have had enough –
border-pinks, clove-pinks, wax-lilies,
herbs, sweet-cress.

O for some sharp swish of a branch –
there is no scent of resin
in this place,
no taste of bark, of coarse weeds,
aromatic, astringent –
only border on border of scented pinks …

O to blot out this garden
to forget, to find a new beauty
in some terrible
wind-tortured place.

H.D. 'Sheltered Garden' (from *Sea Garden*, 1916)

Since the flower garden had been left in abandonment, everything had run wild, and a virgin forest had arisen, a forest of roses over-running the paths, crowded with wild offshoots, so mingled, so blended, that roses of every scent and hue seemed to blossom on the same stem. Creeping roses formed mossy carpets on the ground, while climbing roses clung to others like greedy ivy plants, and ascended in spindles of verdure, letting a shower of their loosened petals fall at the lightest breeze. Natural paths coursed through the wood – narrow footways, broad avenues, enchanting covered walks in which one strolled in the shade and scent. These led to glades and clearings, under bowers of small red roses, and between walls hung with tiny yellow ones. Some sunny nooks gleamed like green silken stuff embroidered with bright patterns; other shadier corners offered the seclusion of alcoves and an aroma of love, the balmy warmth, as it were, of a posy languishing on a woman's bosom.

Émile Zola *La Faute de l'Abbé Mouret* (1875)

The flowers give fragrance, the grass grows, the trees bear,
Fruit overflows, the birds chatter, the river murmurs, the air is cool.
Birds please by voice, the grove by shade, the air by coolness
The fountain by drinking-water, by its murmur the stream, by its flowers the ground.
The murmur of water is charming, the voices of birds are harmonious
The smell of the flowers fragrant, the stream cool, the shade warm.
The beauty of the mentioned place feeds the five senses, were you to note all the marked points together
The water delights the touch, flavour the taste, the bird is
The friend to the ear, and grace to sight, scent to the nose.
The elements are not absent: the earth conceives, the air
Caresses, heat awakens, moisture nourishes.

Matthieu de Vendôme *Ars Versificatoria* (12th century)

An up-hill and down-dale ride of twenty-odd miles through a garish mid-day atmosphere brought him in the afternoon to a detached knoll a mile or two west of Talbothays, where he again looked into that green trough of sappiness and humidity, the valley of the Var or Froom. Immediately he began to descend from the upland to the fat alluvial soil below, the atmosphere grew heavier; the languid perfume of the summer fruits, the mists, the hay, the flowers, formed therein a vast pool of odour which at this hour seemed to make the animals, the very bees and butterflies, drowsy.

Thomas Hardy *Tess of the d'Urbervilles* (1821)

They were wholly one another's now, clasped in each other's arms! They did not kiss, but held each other round the waist, cheek to cheek, united, dumb, delighted with their oneness. Around them bloomed the roses with a mad, amorous blossoming, full of crimson and rosy and white laughter. The living, opening flowers seemed to bare their very bosoms. Yellow roses were there showing the golden skin of barbarian maidens: straw-coloured roses, lemon-coloured roses, sun-coloured roses – every shade of the necks which are ambered by glowing skies. Then there was skin of softer hue: among the tea roses, bewitchingly moist and cool, one caught glimpses of modest, bashful charms, with skin as fine as silk tinged faintly with a blue network of veins. Farther on all the smiling life of the rose expanded: there was the blush white rose, barely tinged with a dash of carmine, snowy as the foot of a maid dabbling in a spring; there was the silvery pink, more subdued than even the glow with which a youthful arm irradiates a wide sleeve; there was the clear, fresh rose, in which blood seemed to gleam under satin as in the bare shoulders of a woman bathed in light; and there was the bright pink rose with its buds like the nipples of virgin bosoms, and its opening flowers that suggested parted lips, exhaling warm and perfumed breath. And the climbing roses, the tall cluster roses with their showers of fine flowers, clothed all these others with the lacework of their bunches, the innocence of their flimsy muslin; while, here and there, roses dark as the lees of wine, sanguineous, almost black, showed amidst the bridal purity like passion's wounds … Not a flower that bloomed the same: the roses differed in the fashion of their wooing. Some, shy and blushing, would show but a glimpse of bud, while others, panting and wide open, seemed consumed with infatuation for their persons. There were pert, gay little things that filed off, cockade in cap; there were huge ones, bursting with sensuous charms, like portly, fattened-up sultanas; there were impudent hussies, too, in coquettish disarray, on whose petals the white traces of the powder-puff could be espied; there were virtuous maids who had donned low-necked garb like demure bourgeoises; and aristocratic ladies, graceful and original, who contrived attractive déshabilles. And the cup-like roses offered their perfume as in precious crystal; the drooping, urn-shaped roses let it drip drop by drop; the round cabbage-like roses exhaled it with the even breath of slumbering flowers; while the budding roses tightly locked their petals and only sent forth as yet the faint sigh of maidenhood.

Émile Zola *La Faute de l'Abbé Mouret* (1875)

Near them there was a large patch of heliotropes, whose vanilla-like breath permeated the air with velvety softness. They sat down upon one of the fallen columns, in the midst of a cluster of magnificent lilies which had shot up there. They had been walking for more than an hour. They had wandered on through the flowers from the roses to the lilies. These offered them a calm, quiet haven after their lovers' ramble amid the perfumed solicitation of luscious honeysuckle, musky violets, verbenas that breathed out the warm scent of kisses, and tuberoses that panted with voluptuous passion. The lilies with their tall slim stems shot up round them with snowy cups, gleaming only with the gold of their slender pistils. And there they rested, like betrothed children in a tower of purity; an impregnable ivory tower, where all their love was yet perfect innocence.

Émile Zola *La Faute de l'Abbé Mouret* (1875)

Coming to kiss her lips (such grace I found,)
Me seemed, I smelt a garden of sweet flowers,
That dainty odours from them threw around,
For damsels fit to deck their lovers' bowers.
Her lips did smell like unto gillyflowers;
Her ruddy cheeks, like unto roses red;
Her snowy brows, like budded bellamoures;
Her lovely eyes, like pinks but newly spread;
Her goodly bosom, like a strawberry bed;
Her neck, like to a bunch of Columbines;
Her breast, like lilies, ere their leaves be shed;
Her nipples, like young blossomed jessamines:
Such flagrant flowers do give most odorous smell;
But her sweet odour did them all excel.

Edmund Spenser Sonnet 64 (from *Amoretti*, 1595)

Through the open door
A drowsy smell of flowers – gay heliotrope,
And white sweet clover, and shy mignonette –
Comes faintly in, and silent chorus lends
To the pervading symphony of peace.

John Greenleaf Whittier 'Among the Hills' (1869)

when the tree begins to flower
like a glimpse of

Flesh

When the flower begins to smell
As if its roots have reached
The layer of
Thirst upon the
Unsealed jar of

Joy

Alice, you should
never sleep under
so much pure pale

so many shriek-mouthed blooms

as if Patience
had run out of

Patience

Alice Oswald 'You Must Never Sleep Under a Magnolia' (2009)

As to the weather it is really heavenly weather. It is too hot for any exertion, but
a breeze lifts at night, and I can't tell you what scents it brings, the smell of a full
summer sea and the bay tree in the garden and the smell of lemons. After lunch
today we had a sudden tremendous thunderstorm, the drops of rain were as big as
marguerite daisies – the whole sky was violet. I went out the moment it was over
– the sky was all glittering with broken light – the sun a huge splash of silver. The
drops were like silver fishes hanging from the trees. I drank the rain from the peach
leaves …

Katherine Mansfield *Letters* (to J. M. Murry, 1920)

Near the violet hills of blooming Hymettus there is a sacred spring and ground soft with fresh turf.

The low woods form a glade; a strawberry tree veils the grass; rosemary, laurel and a black myrtle give out their scents.

And there is a box-tree covered with leaves, delicate tamarisks, fine clovers and an elegant pine tree.

Ovid *Ars Amatoria* (2nd century AD) trans. Dan Draper

There were flowers: delphiniums, sweet peas, bunches of lilac; and carnations, masses of carnations. There were roses; there were irises. Ah yes – so she breathed in the earthy garden sweet smell as she stood talking to Miss Pym who owed her help, and thought her kind, for kind she had been years ago; very kind, but she looked older, this year, turning her head from side to side among the irises and roses and nodding tufts of lilac with her eyes half closed, snuffing in, after the street uproar, the delicious scent, the exquisite coolness.

And then, opening her eyes, how fresh like frilled linen clean from a laundry laid in wicker trays the roses looked; and dark and prim the red carnations, holding their heads up; and all the sweet peas spreading in their bowls, tinged violet, snow white, pale – as if it were the evening and girls in muslin frocks came out to pick sweet peas and roses after the superb summer's day, with its almost blue-black sky, its delphiniums, its carnations, its arum lilies was over; and it was the moment between six and seven when every flower – roses, carnations, irises, lilac – glows; white, violet, red, deep orange; every flower seems to burn by itself, softly, purely in the misty beds; and how she loved the grey-white moths spinning in and out, over the cherry pie, over the evening primroses!

And as she began to go with Miss Pym from jar to jar, choosing, nonsense, nonsense, she said to herself, more and more gently, as if this beauty, this scent, this colour, and Miss Pym liking her, trusting her, were a wave which she let flow over her and surmount that hatred, that monster, surmount it all; and it lifted her up and up when – oh! a pistol shot in the street outside!

Virginia Woolf *Mrs Dalloway* (1925)

By the river he shall know pink willow-herb and purple spikes of loosestrife, and the sweetshop smell of water-mint where the rat dives silently from its hole …

Robert Byron 'All These I Learnt' (1932)

Those herbs which perfume the air most delightfully, not passed by as the rest, but, being trodden upon and crushed, are three; that is, burnet, wild thyme and watermints. Therefore, you are to set whole alleys of them, to have the pleasure when you walk or tread.

Francis Bacon *Of Gardens* (1625)

What wond'rous life in this I lead!
Ripe apples drop about my head;
The luscious clusters of the vine
Upon my mouth do crush their wine;
The nectarine and curious peach
Into my hands themselves do reach;
Stumbling on melons as I pass,
Ensnar'd with flow'rs, I fall on grass.

Meanwhile the mind, from pleasure less,
Withdraws into its happiness;
The mind, that ocean where each kind
Does straight its own resemblance find,
Yet it creates, transcending these,
Far other worlds, and other seas;
Annihilating all that's made
To a green thought in a green shade.
Here at the fountain's sliding foot,
Or at some fruit tree's mossy root,
Casting the body's vest aside,
My soul into the boughs does glide;
There like a bird it sits and sings,
Then whets, and combs its silver wings;
And, till prepar'd for longer flight,
Waves in its plumes the various light.

Such was that happy garden-state,
While man there walk'd without a mate;
After a place so pure and sweet,
What other help could yet be meet!
But 'twas beyond a mortal's share
To wander solitary there:
Two paradises 'twere in one
To live in paradise alone.

How well the skillful gard'ner drew
Of flow'rs and herbs this dial new,
Where from above the milder sun
Does through a fragrant zodiac run;
And as it works, th' industrious bee
Computes its time as well as we.
How could such sweet and wholesome hours
Be reckon'd but with herbs and flow'rs!

Andrew Marvell 'The Garden' (1681)

Late August, given heavy rain and sun
For a full week, the blackberries would ripen.
At first, just one, a glossy purple clot
Among others, red, green, hard as a knot.
You ate that first one and its flesh was sweet
Like thickened wine: summer's blood was in it
Leaving stains upon the tongue and lust for
Picking. Then red ones inked up and that hunger
Sent us out with milk cans, pea tins, jam-pots
Where briars scratched and wet grass bleached our boots.
Round hayfields, cornfields and potato-drills
We trekked and picked until the cans were full,
Until the tinkling bottom had been covered
With green ones, and on top big dark blobs burned
Like a plate of eyes. Our hands were peppered
With thorn pricks, our palms sticky as Bluebeard's.

We hoarded the fresh berries in the byre.
But when the bath was filled we found a fur,
A rat-grey fungus, glutting on our cache.
The juice was stinking too. Once off the bush
The fruit fermented, the sweet flesh would turn sour.
I always felt like crying. It wasn't fair
That all the lovely canfuls smelt of rot.
Each year I hoped they'd keep, knew they would not.

Seamus Heaney 'Blackberry-Picking' (1966)

I love at eventide to walk alone,
Down narrow lanes o'er hung with dewy thorn …
I love to muse o'er meadows newly mown
Where withering grass perfumes the sultry air
Where bees search round with sad and weary drone
In vane for flowers that were but newly there …

John Clare (1793–1864) 'Summer Moods'

But summer is on the wane – the wane. Now M. brings back autumn crocuses, and his handkerchief is full of mushrooms. I love the satiny colour of mushrooms, and their smell and the soft stalks.

Katherine Mansfield *Letters* (to Dorothy Brett, 29th August 1921)

As imperceptibly as grief
The summer lapsed away –
Too imperceptible at last
To seem like perfidy – …

And thus, without a wing
Or service of a keel
Our summer made her light escape
Into the beautiful.

Emily Dickinson 'As Imperceptibly as Grief' (*c*.1895)

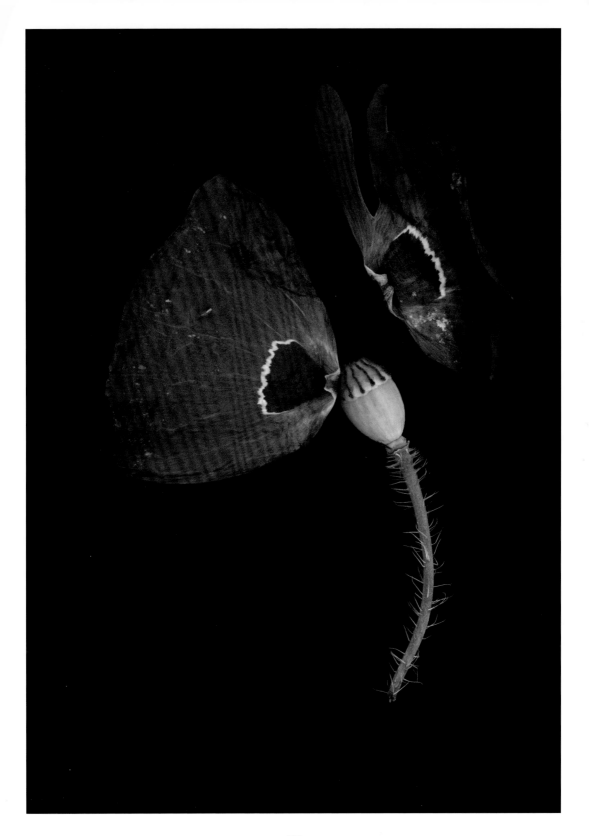

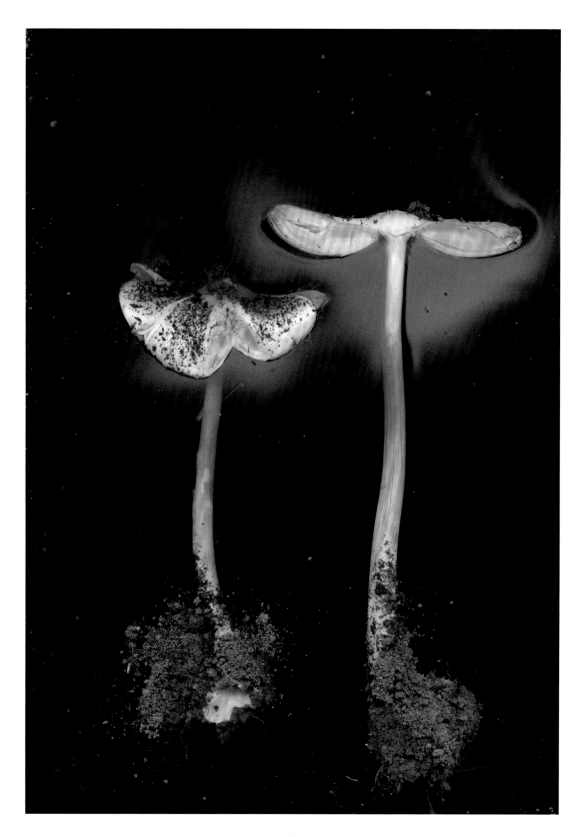

Memory
September

It was Proust who really identified the ambushing nature of smell-memory. Four years before the publication of Proust's *Remembrance of things Past*, Hilaire Belloc wrote in 'On Song', in a book called – perhaps with ironic humility – *On Everything* (1909) the following sentence. 'Song also is the mistress of memory, and though scent is more powerful, a song is more general as an instrument for the resurrection of lost things.' Scent pervades memory but remains invisible. Proust, for whom Belloc and Chesterton had the most prodigious admiration, put it thus: 'But when from a long-distant past nothing subsists, after the people are dead, after the things are broken and scattered, still, alone, more fragile, but with more vitality, more unsubstantial, more persistent, more faithful, the smell and taste of things remain poised a long time, like souls, ready to remind us, waiting and hoping for their moment, amid the ruins of all the rest; and bear unfaltering, in the tiny and almost impalpable drop of their essence, the vast structure of recollection.'

The personal associations that are bound up with scents are notoriously vivid; often smell recall has an almost hallucinatory clarity, usually of events charged with emotion. The emotion comes back first, followed by the memory picture. Nabokov wrote a lot about smell and memory, saying at one point 'nothing revives the past so completely as a smell that was once associated with it.' Both he and Proust believed smell to be a deep reservoir of poetry and he wrote that smell is 'the night light in the bedroom of memory'. Proust was perhaps paramount at delineating house smell, smells indoors, 'linen smells' and 'morning smells', 'natural smells certainly, and coloured by the weather like the countryside outside, but already humanised, homely, confined an exquisite jelly, well made and limpid.' But outside he is busy 'blending all the fruits of the year' and 'balancing the sharpness of hoarfrost with the sweetness of warm bread.'

Autumn smells that I think of are moss, mushrooms, fungus, and ferns.

Celia Lyttelton describes visiting oak moss groves in Morocco where 'the air was powdery and narcotic … giving the impression of fullness a sense of opulence' a sense which we have all got from mossy places in the highlands or pine woods where the effect is heavy and rich and at the same time entirely fresh. Oak moss does not smell like oak, which has the smell of tannin. Tannin is astringent, the term come from '*tanna*', an Old High German word for oak or fir tree, as in *Tannenbaum*. It refers also to the use of wood tannins in tanning animal hides into leather; hence the words 'tan' and 'tanning' for the treatment of leather – as opposed to the tanning shop where the mission is entirely different and also the smell (what an odd smell that is, the smell of fake tan). The tannin compounds are widely distributed in many species of plants, where they play a role in protection from predation. The astringency from the tannins is what causes the dry and puckery feeling in the mouth following the consumption of unripe fruit or red wine. Likewise, the destruction or modification of tannins with time plays an important role in the ripening of fruit and the ageing of wine. It is, somehow, the smell of the shrine, of the ancients, the same smell was cleft from oak with bronze axes. The smell of tanneries and cooperage, of shipwrights and pit props.

It is good to sit inside on short days of the year, often zinc skyed and smelling of little more than zinc, and consider the scents that linger in the mind. Fires, polish, flowers, candlewax, cooking, coffee, bath salts, laundry, fetid vases, airlessness, bad breath, old clothes and shoes, socks especially, musty neglect, dogs, cats, carpets, moths, cobwebs, and poisons in the potting shed. I particularly love the smell of hazel burning, it would be my kindling of choice. When quoting Honor Goodhart's 'Logs to Burn', Richard Mabey says that lilac wood is the most aromatic there is – though it would pain me unbearably to cut one for burning.

By the ends of our lives our heads are full of extinct smell, the extinct smells of childhood. A rotting wooden fence long ago treated with creosote, smelling of tar and decayed earthy mushroom smell. The smell of permanent markers and play-doh. The invigorating turpentine and lemon rind smell of the thuja hedge where we made the den, and nearby it the meaty green leather smell of elder bushes. Hawthorn smelling of honey and fishpaste, fig leaves in the sun smelling of cellulose and an ellipsis of something fruity to do with prunes. Smell memories are different from other memories and the emotions that go with them are different from those that go with other senses. Proust makes the most convincing case for taste and smell as the memory evoking human senses. 'When from long-distant past nothing subsists, after the people are dead, after the things are broken and scattered, taste and smell alone, more fragile but more enduring, more immaterial, more persistent, more faithful, remain poised along time, like souls.'

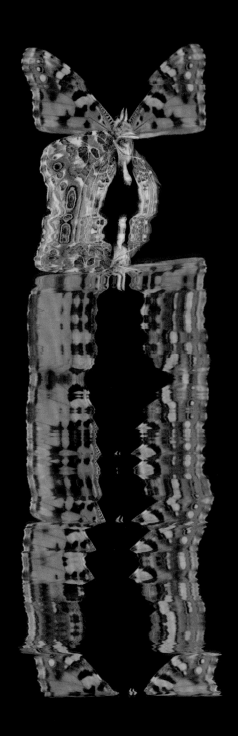

The Sun warms out old memories, the Mist exhumes others, as they intensify the fragrance of trees or the smell of ferns.

Cyril Connolly *The Unquiet Grave* (1944)

The new moon, of no importance
lingers behind as the yellow sun glares and is gone beyond the sea's edge;
earth smokes blue;
the new moon, in cool height above the blushes,
brings a fresh fragrance of heaven to our senses.

D. H. Lawrence 'The New Moon' (1929)

It is yellow in colour, as if it wore a daffodil
tunic, and it smells like musk, a penetrating smell.

It has the perfume of a loved woman and the same
Hardness of heart, but it has the colour of the
Impassioned and scrawny lover.

Its pallor is borrowed from my pallor; its smell
Is my sweetheart's breath.

When it stood fragrant on the bough and the leaves
Had woven for it a covering of brocade,

I gently put up my hand to pluck it and to set it
Like a censer in the middle of my room.

It had a cloak of ash-coloured down hovering over
Its smooth golden body,

And when it lay naked in my hand, with nothing more than
Its daffodil-coloured shift,

It made me think of her I cannot mention, and I feared
The ardour of my breath would shrivel it in my fingers.

Shafer ben Utman al-Mushafi (?–982) 'Quince'

With peach and apricot the garden wall
Was odorous, and the pears began to fall
From off the high tree.

William Morris 'The Earthly Paradise' (1870)

The spirits of the air live on the smells
Of fruit; and Joy, with pinions light, roves round
The gardens, or sits singing in the trees.

William Blake 'To Autumn' (1783)

Tall nettles cover up, as they have done
These many springs, the rusty harrow, the plough
Long worn out, and the roller made of stone:
Only the elm butt tops the nettles now.

This corner of the farmyard I like most:
As well as any bloom upon a flower
I like the dust on the nettles, never lost
Except to prove the sweetness of a shower.

Edward Thomas (1878–1917) 'Tall Nettles'

Now thin mists temper the slow-ripening beams
Of the September sun: his golden gleams
On gaudy flowers shine, that prank the rows
Of high-grown hollyhocks, and all tall shows
That Autumn flaunteth in his bushy bowers;
Where tomtits, hanging from the drooping heads
Of giant sunflowers, peck the nutty seeds;
And in the feathery aster bees on wing
Seize and set free the honied flowers,
Till thousand stars leap with their visiting:
While ever across the path mazily flit,
Unpiloted in the sun,
The dreamy butterflies
With dazzling colours powdered and soft glooms,
White, black and crimson stripes, and peacock eyes,

Or on chance flowers sit,
With idle effort plundering one by one
The nectaries of deepest-throated blooms.

With gentle flaws the western breeze
Into the garden saileth,
Scarce here and there stirring the single trees,
For his sharpness he vaileth:
So long a comrade of the bearded corn,
Now from the stubbles whence the shocks are borne,
O'er dewy lawns he turns to stray,
As mindful of the kisses and soft play
Wherewith he enamoured the light-hearted May,
Ere he deserted her;
Lover of fragrance, and too late repents;
Nor more of heavy hyacinth now may drink,
Nor spicy pink,
Nor summer's rose, nor garnered lavender,
But the few lingering scents
Of streakèd pea, and gillyflower, and stocks
Of courtly purple, and aromatic phlox.

And at all times to hear are drowsy tones
Of dizzy flies, and humming drones,
With sudden flap of pigeon wings in the sky,
Or the wild cry
Of thirsty rooks, that scour ascare
The distant blue, to watering as they fare
With creaking pinions, or – on business bent,
If aught their ancient polity displease, –
Come gathering to their colony, and there
Settling in ragged parliament,
Some stormy council hold in the high trees.

Robert Bridges 'The Garden in September' (from *Short Poems*, 1894)

Pear logs and apple logs,
They will scent your room;
Cherry logs across the dogs
Smell like flowers in bloom,

Honor Goodhart 'Logs to Burn' (1920)

To think that this meaningless thing was ever a rose,
Scentless, colourless, this!
Will it ever be thus (who knows?)
Thus with our bliss,
If we wait till the close?

Though we care not to wait for the end, there comes the end
Sooner, later, at last,
Which nothing can mar, nothing mend:
An end locked fast,
Bent we cannot re-bend.

Christina Rossetti 'Summer is Ended' (1881)

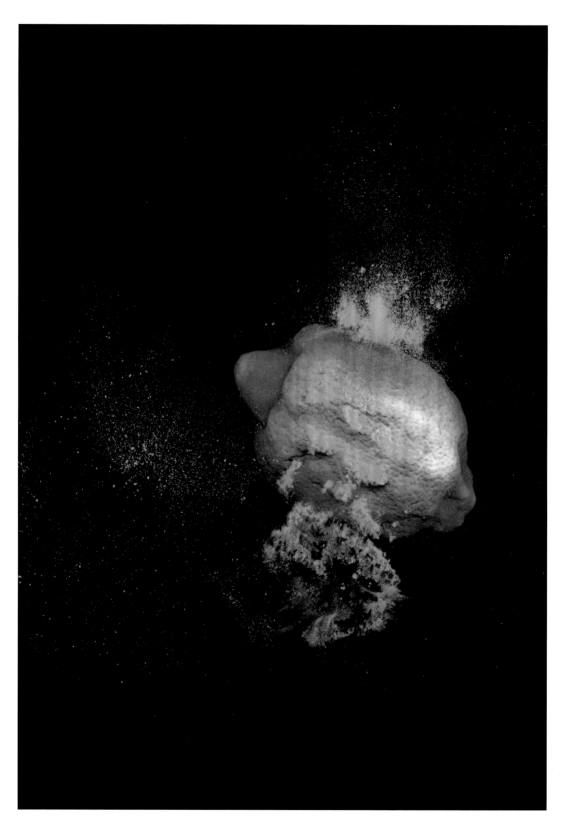

Autumn Decay
October

Of all the seasons Autumn most provokes meditation, philosophising, a drift from description into redolence, to seeing through things as the leaves leave, a shift to elegy. Rilke wrote letters about the coming of autumn in 1907 to Clara, his wife, who was in north Germany when he was in Paris. He describes the 'strong and serious smell which is really the scent of autumn earth. But how glorious is this scent. At no other time it seems to me, does the earth let itself be inhaled in one smell, the ripe earth; in a smell that is in no way inferior to the smell of the sea, bitter when it borders on taste, and more than honeysweet where you feel it is close to touching the first sounds. Containing depth within itself, darkness, something of the grave almost, and yet again of the wind; tar and turpentine and Ceylon tea.' Tea again, such a core smell. Anthony Hecht in 'An Autumnal' writes '… the earthen tea distils at the roots-groins, into the smoky weather A deep familiar essence of the year; A sweet fetor, a ghost of poison, gently welcoming us near.' George Meredith, a hundred years or more earlier, writes 'Earth knows no desolation. She smells regeneration in the moist breath of decay.'

But, once in the open air, she paused. Some emotion – pity, terror, love, but the emotion was strong – seized her, and she was aware of autumn. Summer was ending, and the evening brought her odours of decay, the more pathetic because they were reminiscent of spring. That something or other mattered intellectually? A leaf, violently agitated, danced past her, while other leaves lay motionless. That the earth was hastening to re-enter darkness, and the shadows of those trees …

E. M. Forster *A Room with a View* (1908)

My very heart faints and my whole soul grieves,
At the moist rich smell of the rotting leaves,
And the breath
Of the fading edges of box beneath,
And the year's last rose …

Alfred, Lord Tennyson 'Maud' (1855)

When tuberoses are turning brown they have a human smell.

Émile Zola *Nana* (1880)

He looked and smelt like Autumn's very brother, his face being sunburnt to wheat-colour, his eyes blue as cornflowers, his sleeves and leggings dyed with fruit-stains, his hands clammy with the sweet juice of apples, his hat sprinkled with pips, and everywhere about him that atmosphere of cider which as its first return each season has such an indescribable fascination for those who have been born and bred among the orchards.

Thomas Hardy *The Woodlanders* (1887)

As she came closer to him she noticed that there was a clean fresh scent of heather and grass and leaves about him, almost as if he were made of them.

Frances Hodgson Burnett *The Secret Garden* (1911)

It was when he leant close to me, his little naked torso,
brown and thin, reaching an arm into the row of raspberries,
that I snatched a kiss. The raspberries smelled of rosemary
and among them, like a cuckoo's egg, grew the odd sweetpea …

Mimi Khalvati 'Picking Raspberries with Mowgli' (from *The Weather Wheel*, 2014)

They no longer inhaled the soft languid perfumes of aromatic plants, the musky
scent of thyme and the incense of lavender. Now they were treading a foul-smelling
growth under foot; wormwood with bitter penetrating smell; rue that reeked like
putrid flesh; and hot valerian, clammy with aphrodisiacal exudations. Mandragoras,
hemlocks, hellebores, dwales, poured forth their odours, and made their heads swim
till they reeled and tottered one against the other.

Émile Zola *La Faute de l'Abbé Mouret* (1875)

Today I think
Only with scents – scents dead leaves yield,
And bracken, and wild carrot's seed,
And the square mustard field;

Odours that rise
When the spade wounds the root of the tree,
Rose, currant, raspberry, or goutweed,
Rhubarb or celery;

The smoke's smell too,
Flowing from where the bonfire burns
The dead, the waste, the dangerous
And all to sweetness turns.

It is enough
To smell, to crumble the dark earth,
While the robin sings over again
Sad songs of Autumn mirth.

Edward Thomas 'Digging' (1915)

It was an afternoon which had a fungous smell out of doors, all being sunless and stagnant overhead and around. The various species of trees had begun to assume the more distinctive colours of their decline, and where there had been one pervasive green were now twenty greenish yellows, the air in the vistas between them being half opaque with blue exhalation.

Thomas Hardy *The Hand of Ethelberta* (1876)

Presently, we were aware of an odour gradually coming towards us, something musky, fiery, savoury, mysterious … a hot drowsy smell, that lulls the senses, and yet enflames them, … the truffles were coming.

William Makepeace Thackeray (1811–1863)

Courtesan with hard breast and eye opaque and brown,
That slowly opens like the calm eyes of a steer,
Your thick stem shines like marble, newly cut and clear.

Flower plump and rich, yet odourless, all your renown,
Is in your tempting body, serene as summer skies,
That dully glows, displaying its rare harmonies.

Nor have you flesh like those fair ones who all day
Strew on the summer fields the rows of new mown hay,
Enthroning you, dumb idol, 'midst the incense light.

Thus, the kingly Dahlia, clad in robes of splendour,
Rises without pride his head that has no odour
Disdainfully, among the taunting jasmines white.

Paul Verlaine (1844–1896) 'Dahlia'

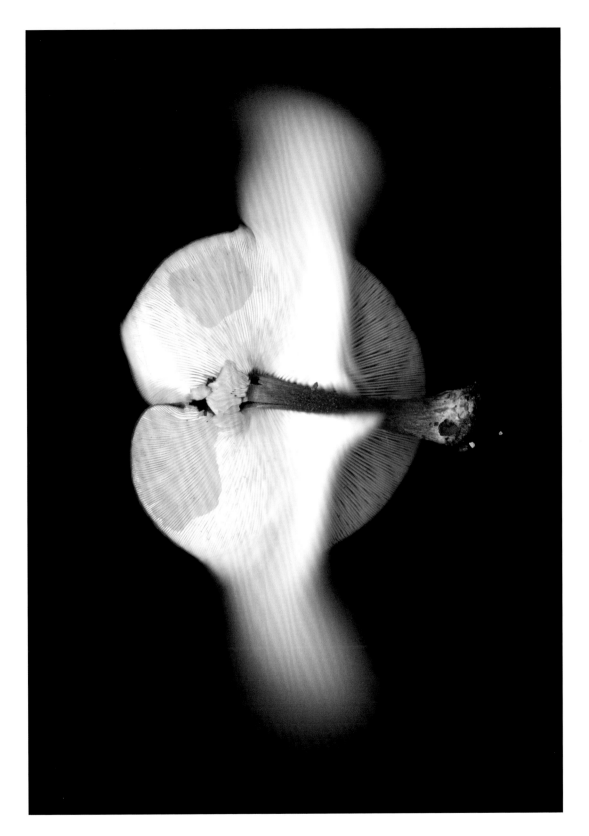

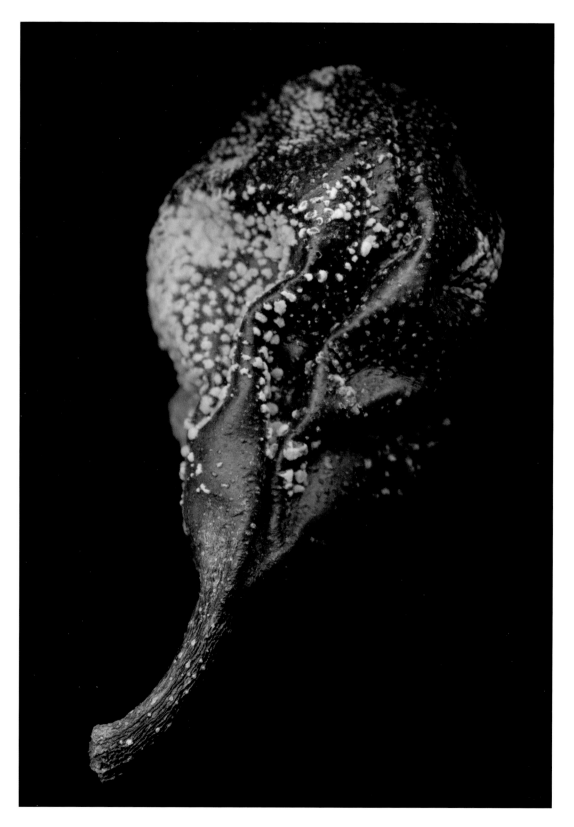

I love you, rotten,
Delicious rottenness.

I love to suck you out from your skins
So brown and soft and coming suave,
So morbid, as the Italians say.

What a rare, powerful, reminiscent flavour
Comes out of your falling through the stages of decay:
Stream within stream.

Something of the same flavour as Syracusan muscat wine
Or vulgar Marsala …

What is it?
What is it, in the grape turning raisin,
In the medlar, in the sorb-apple,
Wineskins of brown morbidity,
Autumnal excrementa;
What is it that reminds us of white gods?

Gods nude as blanched nut-kernels,
Strangely, half-sinisterly flesh-fragrant
As if with sweat,
And drenched with mystery …

So, in the strange retorts of medlars and sorb-apples
The distilled essence of hell.
The exquisite odour of leave-taking. Jamque vale!
Orpheus, and the winding, leaf-clogged, silent lanes of hell …

Medlars, sorb-apples
More than sweet
Flux of autumn
Sucked out of your empty bladders
And sipped down, perhaps, with a sip of Marsala
So that the rambling, sky-dropped grape can add its music to yours,
Orphic farewell, and farewell, and farewell
And the ego sum of Dionysos
The sono io of perfect drunkenness
Intoxication of final loneliness.

D. H. Lawrence 'Medlars and Sorb-Apples' (1923)

Till, on a day roving the field, I chanced
A goodly tree far distant to behold
Loaden with fruit of fairest colours mixed,
Ruddy and gold: I nearer drew to gaze;
When from the boughs a savoury odour blown,
Grateful to appetite, more pleased my sense
Than smell of sweetest fennel, or the teats
Of ewe or goat dropping with milk at even,
Unsucked of lamb or kid, that tend their play.

Milton *Paradise Lost*: Book Four (1667)

I
A spirit haunts the year's last hours
Dwelling amid these yellowing bowers:
To himself he talks;
For at eventide, listening earnestly,
At his work you may hear him sob and sigh
In the walks;
Earthward he boweth the heavy stalks
Of the mouldering flowers:
Heavily hangs the broad sunflower
Over its grave i' the earth so chilly;
Heavily hangs the hollyhock,
Heavily hangs the tiger-lily.

II
The air is damp, and hush'd, and close,
As a sick man's room when he taketh repose
An hour before death;
My very heart faints and my whole soul grieves
At the moist rich smell of the rotting leaves,
And the breath
Of the fading edges of box beneath,
And the year's last rose.
Heavily hangs the broad sunflower
Over its grave i' the earth so chilly;
Heavily hangs the hollyhock,
Heavily hangs the tiger-lily.

Alfred, Lord Tennyson 'A Spirit Haunts the Year's Last Hours' (1830)

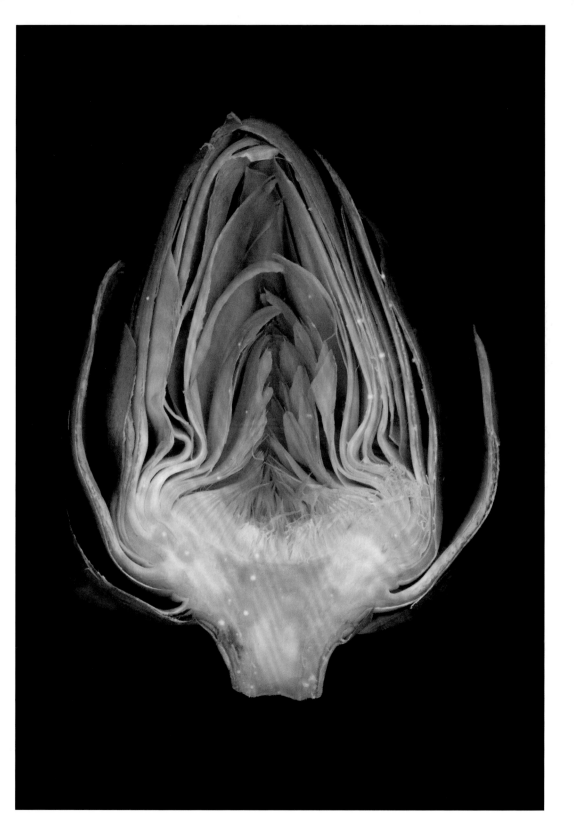

The pounded spise both tast and sent doth please;
In fadinge smoke the force doth incense showe;
The perisht kernell springeth with increase;
The lopped tree doth best and soonest growe.

Gods spice I was, and poundinge was my due;
In fadinge breath my incense favoured best;
Death was my meane my kernell to renewe;
By loppinge shott I upp to heavenly rest.

Some thinges more perfit are in their decaye,
Like sparke that going out geeves clerest light:
Such was my happe, whose dolefull dying daye
Begane my joye and termed fortunes spight.

Robert Southwell (1561–1595) 'Decease Release' ('At Fotheringay')

Men scent out fragrance on the air,
Yet take no heed
Of humble lessons we would read.

Christina Rossetti 'Consider the Lilies of the Field' (1879)

Faint smell of chrysanthemums
Like the smell of a sick ghost …

Hagiwara Sakutarō (1886–1942) 'Cock'

Now from all Parts the swelling Kennels flow,
And bear their Trophies with them as they go:
Filth of all Hues and Odours seem to tell
What Streets they sail'd from, by the Sight and Smell …

Jonathan Swift 'A Description of a City Shower' (1710)

Dying Scents
November & December

One of the pinnacle festivities of the year for me since childhood has always been Guy Fawkes Night, hugely enjoyed across the nation for the unalloyed thrill of rockets and Catherine wheels and above all the smell of cordite. In *The Christmas Chronicles* Nigel Slater encapsulates the return of winter in November … 'We all know winter. The mysterious whiff of jasmine or narcissus caught in the cold air; the sadness of spent, blackened fireworks the morning after Bonfire Night … the magical alchemy of frost and smoke. Winter is the smell of freshly cut ivy or yew …' For sad, and sort of understandable reasons, Bonfire Night has almost been banned in our careless world, yet for those of us who grew up with it as an annual highlight, the prelude to Advent, smoke, and saltpetre are still heady mnemonics. That blue haze that lay on the land after stubble burning is not so far from the blue haze of volatiles emitted from pine forests, giving rise to landmark names such as Smoky Mountains and the Blue Ridge Mountains of Virginia. Not only volatiles create haze and smoke. Pollen grains from catkins and wind-pollinated plants such as grasses are dispersed in their multi billions in spring. I have seen over many springs a sort of fuming, looking like mustard gas, which is pollen pouring into the air from the barely visible male flowers of yew trees. Darwin noticed clouds of pollen from the great forests of North America passing through Alabama in spring. Wind-pollinated plants came first upon the earth, grasses particularly, and have little colour, barely visible flowers, little scent, and vast quantities of pollen. Then, around 120 million years ago, a new pollination strategy developed, and flowering plants first appeared. The real relationship between plants and insects began in the early Cretaceous, with beetle-pollinated gymnosperms such as *Magnolia grandiflora*. It seems likely that beetles led the way in insect pollination, followed by flies. Invertebrates are essential for a lot of plant pollination. Entomophilous plants – those pollinated by insects – produce less pollen, but it is sticky protein laden and such plants must use energy on nectar production and must also communicate with their pollinators somehow: they must advertise, with colour, nectar production – and with scent.

Pollution is a huge factor in inhibiting pollination. A study done by the University of Virginia proved that air pollution is destroying plant fragrance and thereby inhibiting insect pollination. The study estimates that the difference in the number of metres that scent molecules can travel in unpolluted air is between a thousand and two thousand metres as compared with a couple of hundred metres in modern major cities. This is because the volatiles or essential oils emitted by plants react chemically with ozone, hydroxyl and nitrate radicals, and this reaction destroys the smell as we, and more importantly the insects, know it. The study estimates that air pollution is effectively destroying the odour molecules emitted by plants into the air all the time, and by as much as 90 per cent, thus reducing the power of the scent trails used by invertebrates to as little as one tenth of what they were, rather as the smog of dangerous levels of air pollution in cities limits human vision to a few centimetres right in front of them. The internal combustion engines do the same as lightning, reacting with nitrogen in the air. One imagines in former times, without automobiles and heavy industry, smell was at least ten times more noticeable. Hence the 'molestation' of John Gerard's head, Horace Walpole's timidity about the smell of philadelphus, the myth of childhoods smells and of flower smells such as mignonette or evening primrose. It is not so much that the plants no longer smell (apart from those having smell bred out of them) but that scent molecules do not survive in our acrid air, and insects are being forced to travel farther and expend more energy on following scents for forage and procreation.

Absence of smell and development of a 'norm' which is smell-less is what is happening. Just as a world without butterflies is already becoming normal, or without wildflowers, or elephants and tigers. How can we miss what we never knew? So what if a male butterfly of the Danaidae family can no longer travel from flower to flower mixing a cocktail of scents in a pocket on each hind leg until he has created the perfect perfume to attract a female mate? Scent and plants, moths, birds feeding their chicks the grubs of those moths are part of a chain; simple enough, with everything working together for millions of years, entangled, reproducing in cycles, a chain-mail of mythical linkage of which most of us are blissfully unaware.

Now is the time for the burning of the leaves.
They go to the fire; the nostril pricks with smoke
Wandering slowly into a weeping mist.
Brittle and blotched, ragged and rotten sheaves!
A flame seizes the smouldering ruin and bites
On stubborn stalks that crackle as they resist.

The last hollyhock's fallen tower is dust;
All the spices of June are a bitter reek,
All the extravagant riches spent and mean.
All burns! The reddest rose is a ghost;
Sparks whirl up, to expire in the mist: the wild
Fingers of fire are making corruption clean.

Now is the time for stripping the spirit bare,
Time for the burning of days ended and done,
Idle solace of things that have gone before:
Rootless hope and fruitless desire are there;
Let them go to the fire, with never a look behind.
The world that was ours is a world that is ours no more.

They will come again, the leaf and the flower, to arise
From squalor of rottenness into the old splendour,
And magical scents to a wondering memory bring;
The same glory, to shine upon different eyes.
Earth cares for her own ruins, naught for ours.
Nothing is certain, only the certain spring.

Laurence Binyon (1869–1943) 'The Burning of the Leaves'

Afterword: Home, Sensory Perception and the *Umwelt*

I remember a house where all were good
To me, God knows, deserving no such thing:
Comforting smell breathed at very entering,
Fetched fresh, as I suppose, off some sweet wood.
That cordial air made those kind people a hood
All over, as a bevy of eggs the mothering wing
Will, or mild nights the new morsels of Spring:
Why, it seemed of course; seemed of right it should.

Gerard Manley Hopkins (1844–1889) 'In the Valley of the Elwy'

What I find most astonishing and beguiling is that the sense of smell is such a direct molecular combination with bits of the outside world, the substance of our *Umwelt* – a term I picked up on while reading Adam Nicolson's *The Seabirds Cry*. In the study of animal behaviour, this is a twentieth-century German expression – coined by biologist Jakob von Uexküll – for the world as it is experienced by a particular organism: that organism's model of the world, its perception of its environment. I think that we can all recognise that we each live in a 'self-in-world' with subjective reference frames, but we do not often think of this same phenomenon in other creatures. Each living being has its own perceptual milieu, even plants, and the converse of this are the multiple universes perceived from the likewise peculiar perspective of each outside observer. All five senses are key in the mental mapping of our habitual surroundings, our privately developed sense of what and where we are, our personal *Umwelt*. Smell offers us primarily familiar and unfamiliar sensations and this either puts us on our guard or at ease, along with the input of our other senses.

If *Umwelt* is the perceptual world in which an organism exists and acts as a subject, we can build theories of how they experience the world by studying how the senses of various organisms like ticks, sea urchins, amoebae, jellyfish and sea worms, work. In the case of the tick, this eyeless animal finds the way to its watchpoint, at the top of a tall blade of grass, with the help of only its skin's general sensitivity to light. The approach of her prey becomes apparent to this blind and deaf bandit only through the sense of smell. The smell of butyric acid, which emanates from the sebaceous follicles of all mammals, works on the tick as a signal that causes her to abandon her post and fall blindly downward toward her prey. Using an organ sensible to temperature she assesses whether she has been fortunate enough to fall on something warm; if so, she has attained her prey, the warm-blooded animal, and thereafter needs only the help of her sense of touch to find the least hairy spot possible and embed herself up to her head. Thus, for the tick, the *Umwelt* is reduced to only three signals: a specific smell; blood temperature; the glabrous topography of mammals. *Umwelt* has become a philosophic cornerstone of much robotics and machine learning because, if we are to make machines that reason effectively, they are going to have to develop some sort of *Umwelt*, to grapple with the philosophical conundrum of subjectivity and objectivity.

Uexküll's application of the notion of *Umwelt* to the human person has been contested on the grounds of our ability to reason, but it is useful in the context of smell to consider how plants and animals do indeed live in an *Umwelt* – a notion traceable back to Plato, Aristotle and Thomas Aquinas. Among social carnivores it is often important to be aware of each other, aware of those within the tribe as well as prey from outside the tribe, and this requires a level of social cohesion. Professor Thomas Hummel runs a smell clinic in Dresden and his research show that women are typically better at discerning and then recognising in olfactory function. Grown women, boys and girls are all similar in this respect; men lose it at puberty. Hummel posits that women are more interested because they are more aware of smells as social signals, because they are better socially – well, that is his hypothesis. He draws on the observation that women come to his clinic for help because they are upset by the social effects of losing their sense of smell. Men come because they are missing the hedonic effects.

Your sense of smell – like your sense of taste – is part of your chemosensory system (sight, touch and sound being physical senses); your ability to smell comes from specialised sensory cells, olfactory neurons, which are found in a small patch of tissue high inside the nose. These cells connect directly to the brain. Along with taste it is the most direct sense. We smell actual molecules. Smell is most disorderly. Colour and sound are orderly, they come in wavelengths, with a definite hierarchy which is quite straightforwardly visible in a rainbow or a piano keyboard. There is no natural spectrum of smells – no analysis, no categorisation. Smell is also fragile. Both the volatile molecules and the receptor probes are fragile and highly dependent upon precise conditions. Within the nose, mucus is essential to the process and hence the flow of mucus must be constant. At the same time mucus washes away pollutants, irritants and bacteria. In this swirl of molecular and biological contaminants, the receptor cells wear out and must be replaced regularly – about four times a year throughout our lives. This is unlike any other nerve tissue and sadly its efficacy diminishes with age. Because they are 'chemo'-sensory systems, taste and smell therefore operate in a different realm from sight and sound, and require a close contact with the substance of things, with the thing itself, with the volatile fragments of things. The smell of cats, or home. When you breathe and smell your lover's skin, you are taking molecules right inside your body; it is an exchange. In some extraordinary way, what we smell becomes part of us, a fact which makes smell such an intimate sense and such a vulnerable one too, because it is a direct molecular combination with bits of the outside world. All sensory perception is making sense of the world about us, but the olfactory membrane is the only place in the human body where the central nervous system comes into direct contact with the outside world.

Almost more amazing is the fact that inhaling, for example, scents in the garden transcends other multisensorial forms of perception because it generates a psychological process deep in the old emotional part of the brain, where it triggers a series of molecular mechanisms. The effects radiate through the whole body and can produce a feeling of well-being, even of plenitude. One of the profound paradoxes of being a human is that the thick spread of sensation we relish is not perceived directly by the brain, which is blind, deaf, dumb, and unfeeling. 'The brain is silent, the brain is dark', writes Helen Ackerman, '... the brain tastes nothing, the brain hears nothing, the brain smells nothing'. All it receives are electrical impulses, but whereabouts in the brain it receives and interprets is very different for different senses. The body is the transducer, a device that converts energy of one sort into energy of another, electrical impulses, and that is its genius. Proteins bind to odour molecules causing an electrical response which is transmitted directly to the brain's limbic system at the olfactory bulb. There, having checked that the stimuli are real, and having integrated these stimuli with auditory visual information, the olfactory bulb may transmit positive signals to the reward sensors. Hence it has a role in addiction. 'I sing the body electric' wrote Walt Whitman. Our bodies sing with electricity and the brain deftly analyses and considers these impulses as messages that it interprets as soft, supple, curled, dewy, velvety, rose, petal-like. Inhaling is the simplest and most constant connection with our reality, but all reality is subjective reality. Through shamans, seers and ascetics, anchorites, saints, gurus, poets, painters, we grasp for a higher reality, a closer experience, an empathy with other *Umwelts*, other consciousnesses.

Our senses define the edge of consciousness. We are naturally curious, spend lots of our time exploring, testing our senses, which is why we take drugs; go to circuses; listen to loud music; purchase exotic perfumes. We describe ourselves as 'sentient' beings, from the Latin 'to feel'. We have sense perception, and we live on the leash of our senses, which enlarge and at the same time limit and restrain our existence. The balance is very delicate. It is easy for us to take our sense of smell for granted because we exercise it involuntarily: as we breathe, we smell. The sense of smell however is processed in the limbic lobe, one of the oldest parts of the brain and the seat of sexual and emotional impulses, which seems to govern much behaviour and motivation. At birth we appear to have almost no inborn preferences as regards smell, apart from an immediate draw to breast milk. Infants are happy to be fed mashed garlic, as they used to do in Spain. It is conjectured that the stench of cities in former times – rotting refuse, rank faeces and putrefying carcasses (think of a vase of flowers left unemptied over a holiday and multiply it tenfold) – may have been experienced by city dwellers in the background consciousness rather as we now experience traffic noise, which they might have found as an entirely unbearable cacophony.

The sense of smell supplies us unobtrusively with a constant stream of information about our surroundings, homely and unhomely. It tells us about home and family, siblings, mothers, fathers, very strongly in the subconscious. Helen Keller, the first deaf-blind person (let alone woman) to get a Bachelor of Arts degree in the United States, recognised the layers of home smell: '… an old-fashioned country house because it has several layers of odours, left by a succession of families, of plants, of perfumes, and draperies'. She understood the texture and pattern of life, as blind people so often do. Other blind poets in this book, for instance James Joyce, who was almost blind, and most famously Milton. A lot of Helen Keller's writing was simply the first extended eyewitness account of being both blind and deaf. It is interesting that regarding the smell of babies, she wrote that they did not yet have a 'personality scent', those unique odours she could so clearly identify in adults. She was clearly deeply sensual; the illuminating honesty of her descriptions are particularly moving as they were made at a time when this was not easy. And despite her disability, she was more robustly alive than most of her generation and she chose to be a sensualist exploring with everything she had and with the voluptuousness of a courtesan. I particularly remember this description. 'Masculine exhalations are, as a rule stronger, more vivid, more widely differentiate than those of women … In the odour of young men there is something elemental, as of a fire, storm, and salt-sea. It pulsates with buoyancy and desire. It suggests all the things strong beautiful and joyous, and it gives me a sense of physical happiness.' Smell tells you about the age of someone, as it informs your understanding of home, family, siblings, and your kith. Mice, it has been observed, can always tell their kin from non-kin by smell, detecting MHC (major histocompatibility complex) genes, just as it is proven that fish and women can detect these genes in potential sex partners through smell. (It is not an urban myth that being on the pill makes you smell different and may influence your partner relationships.) This is because, not only is inbreeding detrimental, and many sophisticated organisms avoid it through smell, but also offspring from parents with differing MHC genes will have stronger immune systems. Smell tells us much more about the people around us than we generally appreciate. It is designed to tell us about our genetic connection to others. Mothers can identify by body odour their biological children but not their stepchildren. Pre-adolescent children can equally detect full siblings but not half- or step-siblings. We are social beings, and our sense of smell informs us continuously with useful social as well as environmental information. It affects social behaviour; it is meant to.

Smell amplifies our subjective reality, it amplifies the other senses, and it amplifies our emotions on account of the space it occupies in our brain, the seat of its perception, and the limbic system, which is something of an echo-chamber for all perception. An experience in which we engage our sense of smell is a bigger experience. It is a more vivid and often a more pleasurable experience. In childhood all our senses are brighter, brightened too by the dominance of smell among all five, a dominance which we lose later. All the senses are brighter if we use them, and thereby we live more in the present.

What would the world be, once bereft
Of wet and of wildness? Let them be left,
O let them be left, wildness and wet;
Long live the weeds and the wilderness yet.

Gerard Manley Hopkins 'Inversnaid' (1881)

List of Illustrations

Acknowledgements

This book would not have happened without the encouragement of many people who kindly wrote saying how much they had enjoyed the private Christmas version, especially my publisher Jo Christian, but also people who sent really interesting and helpful responses, such as Robert Dalrymple, Mary Keen, Andrew Caldicott, Kate and James Hamilton, Charlie Eustace, Charles Fox, Rosie Pearson and Lucy Snowdon, and Polly Devlin who sent not only encouragement but parcelled up and posted me Mary Oliver's *Devotions*. The hard work of Violet Hudson, the mole who found so much, and on copyright was invaluable; and much thanks for the advice on the same from William Seighart and Rachel Ford. Thanks too for the work of: Dunstan Baker on images and book design; Kate Boxer on mole portraiture; Dan Draper on antique translation; Sarah Mitchell on text; Popeye the pug for his reassuring snoring throughout.

I would also like to thank those poets and writers, including Alice Oswald and Mimi Khalvati, who generously gave permission for the use of their work.

John Betjeman, 'Pot Pourri from a Surrey Garden,' from *Old Lights for New Chancels* (1940). Copyright © Estate of John Betjeman. Reprinted by permission of Hodder & Stoughton.

Cyril Connolly, *The Unquiet Grave* (1944). Copyright © Estate of Cyril Connolly. Reprinted by permission of the estate of Cyril Connolly.

H. D., 'Sea Iris' and 'Sheltered Garden' from *Sea Garden* (1916). Copyright © Estate of Hilda Doolittle. Reprinted by permission of Carcanet Press.

Seamus Heaney, 'Blackberry-Picking' from *Death of a Naturalist*. Copyright © Estate of Seamus Heaney. Reprinted by permission of Faber and Faber, Ltd.

Mimi Khalvati, 'Picking Raspberries with Mowgli' (from *The Weather Wheel*, 2014). Copyright © Mimi Khalvati. Reprinted by permission of Mimi Khalvati.

Giuseppe Tomasi di Lampedusa, *The Leopard*. Copyright © Giangiacomo Feltrinelli Editore, English translation © Harvill and Pantheon Books. Reprinted by permission of Penguin Random House.

Philip Larkin, 'Cut Grass' from *High Windows*. Copyright © Estate of Philip Larkin. Reprinted by permission of Faber and Faber, Ltd.

Alice Oswald, 'You Must Never Sleep Under a Magnolia Tree' from *Falling Awake* (2016). Copyright © Alice Oswald. Reprinted by permission of Alice Oswald.

Alice Oswald, 'Violet' from *Weeds and Wildflowers* (2009). Copyright © Alice Oswald. Reprinted by permission of Alice Oswald.

The Publishers have made every effort to contact holders of copyright works. Any copyright holders we have been unable to reach are invited to contact the Publishers so that a full acknowledgment may be given in subsequent editions.